How to be an Outstanding Trainee Teacher: The Complete Guide

By Mike Gershon

Text Copyright © 2015 Mike Gershon

All Rights Reserved

Series Introduction

The 'How to...' series developed out of Mike's desire to share great classroom practice with teachers around the world. He wanted to put together a collection of books which would help professionals no matter what age group or subject they were teaching.

Each volume focuses on a different element of classroom practice and each is overflowing with brilliant, practical strategies, techniques and activities – all of which are clearly explained and ready-to-use. In most cases, the ideas can be applied immediately, helping teachers not only to teach better but to save time as well.

All of the books have been designed to help teachers. Each one goes out of its way to make educators' lives easier and their lessons even more engaging, inspiring and successful then they already are.

In addition, the whole series is written from the perspective of a working teacher. It takes account of the realities of the classroom, blending theoretical insight with a consistently practical focus.

The 'How to...' series is great teaching made easy.

Author Introduction

Mike Gershon is a teacher, trainer and writer. He is the author of over twenty books on teaching, learning and education, including a number of bestsellers, as well as the co-author of four others. Mike's online resources have been viewed and downloaded more than 2.8 million times by teachers in over 180 countries and territories. He writes regularly for the Times Educational Supplement and has created over 40 guides to different areas of teaching and learning as well as two online courses covering outstanding teaching and growth mindsets. Find out more, get in touch and download free resources at www.mikegershon.com

Training and Consultancy

Mike is an expert trainer whose sessions have received acclaim from teachers across England. Recent bookings include:

- *Growth Mindsets: Theory and Practice*

- *AFL Unlocked: Using Feedback and Marking to Raise Achievement*

- *Success in Linear Assessment: Strategies to Support Learners*

Mike also works as a consultant, advising on teaching and learning and creating bespoke materials for schools. Recent work includes:

- *Improving Literacy and Academic Language*

- *Growth Mindset Assemblies and Pastoral Support Materials*

If you would like speak to Mike about the services he can offer your school, please get in touch by email: mike@mikegershon.com

Acknowledgements

As ever I must thank all the fantastic colleagues and students I have worked with over the years, first while training at the Institute of Education, Central Foundation Girls' School and Nower Hill High School and subsequently while working at Pimlico Academy and King Edward VI School in Bury St Edmunds. Thanks also to all the trainees I have worked with – they always bring an energising set of ideas to the classroom and I have learned as much from them as they have from me.

Other Works from the Same Author

Available to buy now:

How to use Differentiation in the Classroom: The Complete Guide

How to use Assessment for Learning in the Classroom: The Complete Guide

How to use Questioning in the Classroom: The Complete Guide

How to use Discussion in the Classroom: The Complete Guide

How to Teach EAL Students in the Classroom: The Complete Guide

How to be an Outstanding Trainee Teacher: The Complete Guide

How to use Bloom's Taxonomy in the Classroom: The Complete Guide

How to Manage Behaviour in the Classroom: The Complete Guide

More Secondary Starters and Plenaries

Secondary Starters and Plenaries: History

Teach Now! History: Becoming a Great History Teacher

The Growth Mindset Pocketbook (with Professor Barry Hymer)

How to be Outstanding in the Classroom: Raising achievement, securing progress and making learning happen

Also available to buy now, the entire 'Quick 50' Series:

50 Quick and Brilliant Teaching Ideas

50 Quick and Brilliant Teaching Techniques

50 Quick and Brilliant Teaching Games

50 Quick and Easy Lesson Activities

50 Quick Ways to Help Your Students Secure A and B Grades at GCSE

50 Quick Ways to Help Your Students Think, Learn, and Use Their Brains Brilliantly

50 Quick Ways to Motivate and Engage Your Students

50 Quick Ways to Outstanding Teaching

50 Quick Ways to Perfect Behaviour Management

50 Quick Ways to Outstanding Group Work

50 Quick and Easy Ways to Prepare for Ofsted

50 Quick and Easy Ways Leaders can Prepare for Ofsted

50 Quick and Brilliant Ideas for English Teaching (with Lizi Summers)

50 Quick and Easy Ways to Build Resilience through English Teaching (with Lizi Summers)

50 Quick and Easy Ways to Outstanding English Teaching (with Lizi Summers)

Contents

Introduction 11

Chapter One – What Is Teaching All About? 15

Chapter Two – What Is Learning All About? 35

Chapter Three – Becoming a Teacher 53

Chapter Four – Understanding Learners 71

Chapter Five – Unpicking the Lesson 87

Chapter Six – Facilitation vs Instruction 105

Chapter Seven – Sustaining Pace and Challenge 121

Chapter Eight – Learning From Yourself; Learning From Others 137

Chapter Nine – Communicating 155

Chapter Ten – From A to B – Creating the Environment for Progress 173

Conclusion – In The Beginning There Was The Lesson 191

Select Bibliography 195

Introduction

Hello and welcome to *How to be an Outstanding Trainee Teacher: The Complete Guide*. This book has everything you need to excel in the classroom and get your career off to a flying start. It's a practical, critical and reflective handbook which gives you the tools to make incredible progress during your training.

Teaching is a fantastic job. It's rewarding, stimulating and, as the old saying goes, no two days are ever the same.

It's also challenging, and that challenge is what makes it both difficult and deeply satisfying to master. After all, there can be little satisfaction gained from excelling at something easy. You know this, of course. Given the options available you must do – because I know one of the reasons you've gone into teaching is to face and meet that challenge!

The teacher has myriad things they have to balance – the needs of their students, the demands of the curriculum and the uncertainty of how any particular lesson will play out (children and young adults being somewhat unpredictable!). Getting the balance right is tricky – but it's a lot of fun as well.

I remember starting training myself, a few years ago now. The intermingling of excitement, anticipation and mild trepidation comes back to me as I sit writing. My mind wanders to those first few formative months in the classroom, standing on the opposite side of the divide; seeing the lesson from the inside, rather than the outside I'd been used to at school.

But enough about me! This book is about you. About your training, your career and your future.

I want you to be a brilliant teacher. I want you to ace your training. And I want you to finish the year looking forward to your career, well-placed to become a superb professional; a leader in the classroom who consistently gets the best out of their students and makes learning happen, no matter the circumstances.

So how are we going to do this? Well, I can't be there with you all of the way, observing your lessons and giving you feedback. Would that I could! But this is the next best thing. A step-by-step handbook you can use to underpin, guide and enhance everything you do during your training – whether that training is a PGCE, a school-based route or something else.

My aim is to distil teaching wisdom (my own and other people's) into a series of ten chapters, each of which will help you to think critically about what teaching involves, to reflect on your own ideas and experiences and, crucially, to achieve practical success in the classroom.

I'm not going to give you every single thing there is to know about outstanding teaching. That would be too much. Instead, I'm going to tailor the advice, ideas and guidance so it fits with the stage you are at, helping you to become an outstanding trainee. Someone who plans brilliant lessons, quickly builds rapport, manages behaviour effectively and, most of all, motivates and inspires their students.

I have written the book with the intention that it be read straight through. Each chapter builds on the last. However, how you use it is up to you. And there is certainly no harm in diving into the chapters which most interest you from the get go.

Every chapter comes with a set of questions and activities at the end. These are designed to help you think critically about your teaching practice – and to reflect on your previous experiences of education, along with the assumptions and ideas to which these might give rise.

One way you might like to use the book is to read it through before you begin your training, and then to return to it during the course of the year. This will give you a firm grounding in what makes an outstanding trainee teacher while also allowing you to contextualise the information in relation to your classroom experiences.

Every chapter contains practical ideas you can either build on or take away and start using immediately. This is a theme through all of my work on teaching, learning and education. We are in a practical job and the gap between theory/evidence/research and actual teaching always needs to be bridged.

So, let me give you a quick rundown of what you can expect to find in the chapters which follow.

Chapters 1 and 2 focus on unpicking teaching and learning, looking at each in turn. The aim is to get underneath two ideas with which you will be familiar and think about them in a more critical way. A series of different answers to the questions 'What is teaching all about?' and 'What is learning all about?' are presented. These will broaden and deepen your understanding at the same time as they encourage you to reflect on and analyse what you already know.

Chapters 3 and 4 look at what it means to be a teacher and how we can begin to understand the learners with who we work. These chapters build on the first two. They give a clear insight into what makes an outstanding trainee teacher and explain why understanding the children or young adults you teach is vitally important if you want your teaching to be effective.

Chapters 5, 6 and 7 look at the unit through which all our teaching takes place: the lesson. Here we examine different approaches you can take and the practical results of these, as well as the tools and techniques you can call on to ensure your lessons are as good as possible.

In Chapter 8 we think about the process of learning you go through during your training year and beyond. Here we are concerned with how best to maximise the insights you gain from the mistakes you make, the observations you do and the advice you receive. In essence, this chapter is about you maximising your own progress by taking control of your training and development.

Chapters 9 and 10 focus on the fundamental attributes outstanding teachers possess and which you are aiming to develop. Chapter 9 looks at communication in the classroom, analysing how we question, how we explain and how we manage behaviour. The chapter as a whole is concerned with what we can do to ensure our communication is as effective as possible, because this helps to raise achievement. Chapter 10 draws matters to a close by looking at progress and thinking about what outstanding teachers do to ensure their classroom is an environment in which everybody can make exceptional progress, regardless of their starting points.

And there you have it!

A step-by-step guide to becoming an outstanding trainee teacher, containing everything you need to excel, to teach great lessons and to make great learning happen.

All that remains is for me to wish you good luck! I'm sure you'll do a fantastic job during your training and go on to become a brilliant teacher who engages and motivates students left, right and centre. The very fact that you are reading this book illustrates your commitment to being outstanding. Take on board the ideas and strategies which follow, apply them to your teaching, reflect on the results, adapt and modify as necessary and, I have no doubt, you will swiftly become an indispensable member of any school you are a part of – whether as a trainee or, a little further down the line, a fully paid-up member of the profession.

So read on and enjoy – and if we happen to bump into each other during the course of our careers, come and say 'hi' and tell me how you're getting on. I'm sure you'll be doing great.

Chapter One – What Is Teaching All About?

So we start at the beginning, where all good stories begin. And this is a story of a sort. Your story. The story of your training; of your career; perhaps of a significant part of your future life. However much of your time teaching comes to take up, though, it will be a story all the same. A story of growing and developing; of change and progression.

So we begin at the beginning, with a simple question. One to which I know you will already have an answer, predicated on your own beliefs, experiences and learning.

All I want to do here is present you with a range of possible answers about what teaching may be. My aim is not to place a stake in the ground and attach a board to it which reads: This is teaching and may no more be said!

Rather, I would like to unpack the question by providing a series of different answers; a plurality, if you will. This, I hope, will serve two ends.

First, it will point to the many facets which go to make up teaching. Facets which are of greater or lesser importance depending where you work and how you view the profession.

Second, it will intimate that teaching is, in many senses, a highly personal job. Aside from the central, unarguable tenets that teaching concerns the transmission of knowledge and the facilitation of learning, there are many different paths down which an answer to the question 'What is teaching all about?' can lead.

Now let me lead you down some of those paths.

A General Answer to the Question

In general we can say, without much controversy, that teaching concerns learning, knowledge and understanding. The former is constructed through the development of the latter. The teacher's role is to help their students to learn. In doing this they broaden and deepen both their knowledge and understanding.

This is a process which has existed for thousands of years; upon which, it could be argued, much of human civilisation is built.

Yet, in our current situation, in the twenty-first century, teaching has both a general and a bureaucratic meaning. I say bureaucratic because a significant proportion of the teaching which takes place in the world is a direct function of decisions made by states. That is, education is seen as a public good, provided to citizens and subjects in most countries under the auspices of the state. Of course, much formal education exists outside of this context as well. But even then, such as in privately-funded schools or schools supported by charities independent of state control, a degree of bureaucracy remains.

We could term this in another way.

Teaching is now a profession, highly regarded and possessed of its own body of knowledge concerning what that profession entails and how one may come to be skilled at it.

There are two aspects to the general answer then:

First, teaching is an ancient tradition intimately tied up with the transmission of culture, including the attendant knowledge which goes to make up some or all of that culture.

Second, teaching is a modern profession interwoven with the organisations and individuals who provide and control the means for it to take place.

Teaching is both a familiar activity arising out of human beings' desire to communicate and to pass on information and skills and a less familiar activity (to those outside or entering the profession) concerned with the formalisation of that process for the benefit of individuals and wider society.

Thinking in this way helps us to see that everyone entering the profession does so with extensive prior experience of teaching and learning, but that this may have come largely while in the role of student and may not fall neatly into one or the other of the categories, instead straddling them both.

Training to teach therefore involves, to no small extent, a critical reflection on the existing assumptions we have about what teaching means and what constitutes learning. To not do this risks failing to take account of the fact that our previous experiences of teaching and learning may not constitute experiences of what these two things can be when at their best.

A brief example will illustrate the point.

Research (Hattie, *Visible Learning;* Black et al *Assessment for Learning: Putting it into Practice*) suggests that feedback is far more effective than grades in helping students to make progress. Feedback means telling students what they have done well and what they need to do to improve.

Put this way the point is obvious.

However, if our own experience of teaching and learning is heavily bound up with the giving and receiving of grades without or in lieu of feedback, we might struggle to break the conceptual habit this will have unconsciously formed unless we reflect on it directly.

As we will see later on in the book, certain elements of effective teaching run counter to received wisdom and past experience. Their implementation rests, in part, on us looking critically at our existing understanding of what, in general, teaching is.

Teaching is Communication

So let me put a proposition to you:

Teaching is communication. Nothing more and nothing less.

What are your thoughts? Do you agree? Why?

The clearest criticism of the proposition is that it is so general as to be relatively useless in analytical terms. It is a platitude voicing something self-evident.

But what would it mean to view teaching primarily through the lens of communication?

First we would need to define the term rather more precisely.

By communication I mean the interactions which take place between teachers and students, as well as those which take place between students. These interactions include speaking, listening, reading and writing, as well as non-verbal communication, visual communication independent of body language (such as a diagram) and the pieces of meaning which can be read into all the above (to give a literary metaphor, the subtext).

This delineation increases the utility of the proposition. Now we are thinking about how teaching, at root, rests on the communication, in all its forms, which happens in the classroom as well as, at times, outside of it (consider, for example, the teacher sat in the staff room marking students' work – here communication is taking place without the student being on hand).

It follows that, if we tentatively accept the proposition, the quality of teaching, and by extension learning, will connect directly to the quality of communication which takes place between teacher and student or between different students.

But what do we mean by quality?

Again, we can develop the specifics of a broad concept.

Quality of communication encompasses the manner in which the teacher conveys information, the types of questions they ask, the relevance and sharpness of the feedback they give, the manner in which they talk to students, the body language through which they convey (or fail to convey) authority, openness, support, enthusiasm and professionalism, the dialogue which takes place between students, including the extent to which this is critical, focussed and based on the topic of study, and the expectations the teacher exudes both implicitly and explicitly every time they interact with an individual student, a group or the whole class.

Now the proposition starts to take on a more nuanced, deeper meaning. Teaching is communication. Communication encompasses the interactions outlined above. The quality of those interactions can vary. Higher quality interactions, with quality at least loosely defined, are preferred in all cases.

Thinking about teaching in this way helps us to attend closely to how we communicate and what we communicate, as well as to how students communicate and the content of their communication.

It causes us to think about the information which is continually passing between us and our students, as well as that which passes between pairs, groups or the whole class during the course of our teaching.

We can then start to consider how to ensure the information we convey – written, verbal or visual – is suited to our ends, and how we can use the information students convey to teach better (for example, by asking more accurate questions or by adapting our lessons to meet the needs of the pupils in front of us).

You and the Students

Some would argue that here we have come to the crux of what teaching is really all about: the relationship between you and your students.

As with the idea of teaching as communication, this aspect of the job fits closely with the point we made earlier about teaching being a human behaviour with a long and ancient history. A behaviour which originates, perhaps, in the passing on of knowledge from one generation to the next in order to increase the chances of survival.

Of course, in the modern world the division of labour permits that formal schooling is conducted by experts, leaving family members free to work and also enhancing, generally, the likelihood that children and young adults will learn more and become better educated than would otherwise be the case.

This means that as teaching professionals we do not have any prior attachment to the students we teach – differentiating the job from the imagined familial genesis outlined above.

The consequence of this is simple.

Teaching is about building and maintaining good relationships with our students. Doing this helps overcome the lack of attachment, therefore enabling us to fulfil a role which nature might otherwise dictate as being reserved for parents and kin.

Often, part of the relationship building is done for us. The culture in which we live values education and believes in showing respect to others, particularly those in positions of authority who have the express intention of helping us, leading to a situation where students arrive predisposed to view teachers positively.

However, this is not always the case. And, we might also note that even with a strong starting point we still have to put effort into developing and sustaining relationships.

As you may remember from your own school days, supply teachers often get a hard time of it from the students they are asked to teach. This is often because they have no prior relationship with them.

Why would they?

Their job is to cover lessons at short notice, when people are sick or away on leave.

They have had no chance to get to know the students in question – to develop any sense of rapport. As likely as not it will be the first time they have seen them. Even getting to grips with names will prove tricky.

Compare this to a different scenario: a teacher at school, college or university with whom you had a good working relationship. They knew your name. They knew a little bit about you. They knew where you were at with your work and what you needed to do to improve. Importantly, you probably knew what to expect from them; and this ability to predict and anticipate allowed you to enjoy their lessons more, to look forward to them and to get more work done.

From this angle, teaching is driven by the positive relationships teachers are able to establish with their students. If no such relationships can be cultivated, the rest of the task will be extremely hard to achieve – for everybody.

Creating Lessons

But what is that task?

We have our general answer above. Yet it remains to be seen how this (helping students to develop their knowledge and understanding and, by extension, to learn) plays out in practice.

Outside the confines of the classroom, teaching can be viewed as both singular and multifaceted. Singular because all teaching shares the same general basis. Multifaceted because it can take many forms. A parent showing a child how to tie a shoelace, for example. Or a manager talking a junior colleague through the process of delivering an appraisal before inviting them to sit in on one and then try it out for themselves.

Inside the classroom, teaching becomes somewhat more homogenous in terms of form, if not in terms of the content, style and delivery which fills that form.

The basic unit through which most professional teachers work is the lesson.

This is partly defined by administrative considerations – the division of the school day and timetabling matters – partly by tradition, and partly by the continued efficacy of the lesson as a unit into which learning can be placed.

Lessons have a beginning and an end. They are discrete blocks of time which give teacher and students the opportunity to focus on a shared goal to the benefit of all concerned (at least, they do in an ideal world!).

That goal is defined by the teacher, usually with reference to a wider curriculum provided by the school or central government. (Notice how here we again see that interweaving of teaching as an interaction between teacher and students and teaching as a bureaucratically-informed exercise).

All this means that teaching is about creating lessons. A curriculum is prescribed for children of a given age, in relation to given subjects. The level of flexibility within this curriculum varies depending on the age of the child and the mores of the issuing state or institution. The teacher's role is to interpret the curriculum for their charges.

They do this by creating lessons.

These lessons underpin the communication which takes place between teachers and students.

They are the structure upon which learning sits.

As we noted, the style, delivery and content of lessons can vary wildly. But their essential purpose – the role they play in the teaching process – hardly ever varies. The lesson is the space in which teaching takes place. It is the form of that learning. The vessel into which we pour our content, our ideas, our concepts, processes, skills and so forth.

Planning lessons is thus one of the most important skills any budding educator needs to develop. And we will attend to this in due course.

For now, you might like to reflect on a couple of questions – one fairly concrete and linked to your past experience, the other rather more speculative…

Looking back on your own experiences of schooling, to what extent did the structure of the school day circumscribe your learning?

And, if lessons didn't exist, how else might teaching and learning be structured?

Facilitating Progress

Lessons are where learning takes place. They are created and delivered by teachers, whose aim is…what, exactly?

Well, there may be various answers to this question. But one to which there is widespread agreement runs as follows:

The aim of creating and teaching lessons is to help students learn as much as possible. By learning as much as possible, they make progress. That is, they know more and are able to do more than was previously the case. Great teachers maximise progress — they help all of their students to learn as much as possible.

Teaching becomes all about progress: the progress students can make while they are in the classroom.

That there are countless ways in which progress can be facilitated is beyond dispute. That there are better and worse ways is slightly more contentious. Certainly, research evidence (and again, we will come to this in more detail later) exists which gives strong support to specific classroom strategies and techniques.

Yet, teaching been an art rather than a science means that no definitive method, based on proven and immutable laws, presently exists. And nor is it ever likely to.

With that said, we are not descending into absolute relativism here. Some things are better than others, that much is clear. This might be because they are supported by evidence, because they are underpinned by sound reasoning, or because they are logically deducible from certain premises.

Because of the practical nature of teaching, and the inherent uncertainty over what will work best with who and in what context, trial and error is an important part of the job.

This is never truer than in your first few years; especially while you are training.

Students are not objects, they are subjects. Unlike atoms or celestial bodies, their behaviour can be difficult to predict. They have wills, motives, desires and intentions. These — solely or in combination — cause them to act in ways familiar, unfamiliar and, sometimes, long forgotten. (See if you can dredge up any memories of some of your own actions as a child or, better yet, a teenager. It is likely these vignettes will stand in stark contrast to the rather more sober and upright self you now present.)

To facilitate progress – to *maximise* progress – we need to develop a repertoire of effective teaching tools. These include strategies, activities and techniques. Developing such a suite of tools requires a fair amount of trial and error. Ideally, we begin from evidence, example and sound reasoning. But then we need to test whatever follows in the heat of reality. Not just to see if it works, but also to see how we might need to adapt it for our own teaching style and for the students which whom we are working.

Making Mistakes

It took Edison a long time to invent the lightbulb. One story, possibly apocryphal, quotes him as saying he found 10,000 ways the light bulb would not work, all of which lead him to the method which proved successful.

The tale illustrates the importance of failure – and of making mistakes – to any undertaking in which the ultimate goal is to be successful; particularly an undertaking of a practical kind, such as the development of a new product or, indeed, teaching.

That teaching is a practical activity goes without saying. In fact, it is one of the features which attracts many to the profession. Of course, this sense of practical endeavour is underwritten by intellectual work, but the practical focus always remains. It is this, after all, which describes the actual act of teaching – of delivering a lesson.

Making mistakes is an important part of how we learn. This is easy to remember (and experience) in the kitchen, on the sports field or while learning to drive.

It is perhaps harder to keep in mind – maybe even to accept – when one is engaged in a professional activity.

But great teaching relies on mistakes.

Or, to put it another way, great teaching relies on the teacher spotting, reflecting on, analysing and using their mistakes.

This sets the issue in a slightly different light.

Every time we plan a lesson we are creating something which does not yet exist. How do we know whether it will work?

Answer: We don't.

Every time we teach a lesson to a class, how do we know whether or not they will respond to it as we predict?

Answer: We don't.

In both cases, experience can undoubtedly play a big part, but even the most experienced teachers make mistakes or find themselves surprised by new characters, group dynamics and unexpected responses.

This means that teaching is as much about making mistakes as it is about getting things right. Turn this around and we see that getting things right will usually be a function of getting things wrong first (and maybe second, third and fourth) time around, reflecting on this and then applying our learning in the future.

Teaching involves continuous adjustments – during lessons, during planning and while marking. These adjustments can be difficult to gauge at first. This is natural and to be expected. If you find yourself in this position, do not be disheartened.

Fine-tuning the adjustments becomes easier the more mistakes you make, providing you set out with the aim of learning from these.

It is, in fact, rather as Oscar Wilde put it: 'Experience is the name everyone gives to their mistakes.'

Assessing Learning

We mentioned the facilitation of progress as one of our answers to the question: What is teaching all about? What we didn't do there is consider how we actually come to measure progress. And, if we do not have a means of so doing, progress becomes a concept which is ungrounded. It floats on the breeze; lacks relevance; becomes impossible to pin down.

Seen from this angle, teaching is primarily concerned with assessing learning. The teacher's job is to see what students know, what they don't know and to then use this information as the basis of their attempts to bridge the gap.

We can assess learning in a few different ways.

First, we have the formal assessments we all remember – GCSEs, SATS, A Levels. These measures have a younger sibling called in-class assessments – essays, questions, project work set by the teacher.

Second, we can ask questions. This form of assessment can be written or verbal. It will not have escaped your attention that it tends to form part of the first type of assessments as well. Most exam papers consist of a series of questions, to be answered in timed conditions.

I draw out questions as a separate category because questioning is such a vital part of the teacher's toolkit. Through questions we are able to draw out information at almost any point; they are always there, ready to be deployed for the purposes of assessing learning (as well as making students think, with these two purposes often overlapping).

We will look at questioning in depth later on. Here, let me just say that as teachers we tend to ask hundreds of questions every day. Yet the quality of those questions is unlikely to be uniformly high unless we attend to their subject, their structure and the type of answers they invite students to give.

Our third and final means of assessing learning is the general elicitation of information. This is not mutually exclusive from the previous two ways. In fact, it can encompass both of them, as well as much else besides.

Eliciting information includes setting and marking formal assessments and asking questions. It also involves listening to students, reading their work, observing them in class, using techniques which allow the entire class to show you their thinking at the same time (such as mini-whiteboards) and anything else which gives you access to what students think, know, understand and can do.

Looking back, you will see that we have moved from the specific to the general in trying to unpick what it means to say teaching is about assessing learning.

Not only does this serve to show why assessing learning might be thought of as such an important concept, it also illustrates how any interaction with students or the work students produce is an opportunity to assess (in the broad sense) where they are at. And of course, we can then use this information to inform our teaching – ensuring that what we do matches the needs of our learners as closely as possible.

Opening Students' Eyes

If we have a good understanding of where our students are at, we are in a better position to teach them.

If the opposite is true, we may find ourselves teaching lessons which rehash old ground students are already familiar with.

When looked at in an ideal sense, teaching and learning tend not to be concerned with this. Rather, the aim is to open the student's eyes, helping them to see things which were previously obscured or, perhaps, not visible at all.

In Plato's famous story, the philosopher uses the analogy of shadow figures dancing on the wall of a cave to illustrate the way in which what we think we see or know about the world may turn out to be other than it seems.

In Plato's cave, the dancing figures are shadows created by the flames of the fire. It is only when the teacher – philosopher in this case – intervenes, that the people watching the cave wall find themselves drawn outside, into the light. Here, their eyes are opened and the world appears to them, anew and afresh.

Forgive me for shortening and somewhat bastardising Plato's intricate allegory about the nature of appearance and reality. But this has been done with good intentions! (Whether that alone is enough to warrant such changes is a discussion we can leave for another time.)

The imagery serves to neatly demonstrate how teaching can influence our students' perspective; the lenses through which they see the world.

Opening students' eyes means presenting them with information and ideas they would otherwise miss, or come to find through more circuitous means – or by chance, if at all. This ranges from the simple act of teaching new concepts such as nuclear fusion or identity (depending on the age group) to the slightly more complex act of problematizing students' present understanding (such as when we revisit ideas or information learned at an earlier age) and through to the challenging of views or opinions via the provision of quite different ways of thinking, or the introduction of previously undiscovered problems.

In all these cases the aim is the same: to develop students' minds by giving them new experiences.

This can be exciting and confusing. It can be invigorating and challenging.

Some students may resist it; others will embrace it, sometimes with great fervour.

Why not take this opportunity to think back to a time when a teacher or lecturer opened your eyes? What was it like? Try to think yourself into the frame of mind you had at the time. How did it feel to have a new vista laid out in front of you? Or to have a firmly-held belief challenged?

Now, consider what your mind might be like if such an instance had never occurred. If you had never experienced the contrasting perspective or if someone had never unlocked a door to another chamber of thought for you.

And now consider what else might be out there, waiting to be discovered.

And then think about how many opportunities you will have to give this experience to your students, through the lessons you teach.

Passing on Knowledge

Another way to think about teaching is a touch more prosaic than the enlightenment trope underpinning the idea of opening students' eyes.

Passing on knowledge can sound somewhat dry and uninspiring in comparison to the prospect of enhancing a student's understanding of what it means to be human or showing them for the first time how surface tension holds water together, seemingly miraculously, on the exterior of a leaf.

But we must always remember that knowledge is the bedrock upon which learning and development rest.

A student who cannot recite their six times table is not in a position to use this knowledge to make swift calculations further down the line.

And when we take ourselves right back to the first years of schooling, what do we find?

The very beginnings of knowledge transmission. Beginnings upon which so much else rests: the first steps in reading and writing.

Language is a tool humans have developed. It has been passed on through generations. The alphabet is a set of arbitrary symbols which possess meaning because we credit them with meaning. And where does this crediting come from?

We are not born with it.

It has to be learned.

To illustrate the case, we can turn to an alternative set of symbols: здравствуйте.

You may know Russian and recognise the symbols as belonging to the Cyrillic script. Or, like me, you may not. (I used Google Translate to translate 'hello' into Russian.)

At this fairly advanced stage of our development – a stage when we can read text like this and make sense of it – it is natural to take for granted the fact that everything we are able to do stems, initially, from the passing on of knowledge concerning the alphabet. Without having first been given access to that knowledge, we would not have been able to take the next step, then the next and so on.

Thus, the transmission of knowledge is, arguably, what teaching is really all about. If knowledge if not transmitted, it may wither and die; as happens with certain languages as the last remaining speakers come to pass away.

But let us move away from these forebodings and turn back to something we mentioned earlier: the curriculum.

It is here that we find the most cogent proof for our suggestion that teaching centres on the transmission of knowledge. When we create our lessons, we do so with the curriculum in mind. Our aim is to teach students the content of that curriculum over a series of sessions (which could last for as long as three or four years).

In doing this, we find ourselves intimately involved with the transmission of knowledge. The curriculum, that careful delineation of relevant content, represents a stock of accumulated knowledge deemed apt and appropriate for students of a given age studying a given course or programme of study. It is from here that our lessons begin; it is from here that we decide how we will transmit that which our culture has already established as being of value.

Acculturation

And so we come to our last answer to the question 'What is teaching all about?'

Acculturation.

The term has a few meanings. Here, we are interested in its use to describe the process by which we adopt the behaviour patterns of our surrounding culture. A similar term is socialisation, meaning to learn the norms and values of the culture in which we find ourselves.

There is a tension here because we may find ourselves in a multicultural society or a multicultural classroom, in which different cultures, and therefore potentially different norms and values, sit side-by-side. The tension arises from the risk which is posed by us assuming that our own culture is right and all else wrong, or that our own culture is inherently or implicitly better or more worthy than others.

Once more, I do not advocate a descent into moral relativism here, whereby we say everything is equal and no judgements can be made. Rather, I am indicating the potential biases and unfavourable judgements we might fall into if we are not alive to the possibility.

With that said, let us think a little about acculturation.

Teaching, one could argue, involves the teacher helping their students to become fully-fledged members of the society to which both belong. In doing this, they must introduce those students to at least some of the norms and values necessary to achieve this, as well as knowledge and understanding the society has deemed important and worthy of study.

Comparison will again allow us to see this point more sharply. See if you can get hold of a curriculum from a country other than the one in which you are training to teach. You can do this quickly by searching online. Compare this to the curriculum you are or will be using.

Notice the overt content of the curricula and how this is similar in places and very different in other areas. Notice too how the implicit messages of the curricula diverge. This is because they are underpinned by different norms and values, with these being closely associated with the prevailing trends, customs, traditions and beliefs in the society from which they come. Certainly there will be overlaps between the two curricula in these areas – but so too will there be major differences.

This serves to show how teaching is no small part about the acculturation or socialisation of students who are slowly making their way from the safe and supportive confines of the family unit out into the wider world – a world they must appreciate and understand if they are to have a chance of succeeding in it.

And so we find ourselves back where we began, faced by the question: What is teaching all about?

By now you will have seen that my presentation of a whole series of answers has been a way of giving a broader answer. Namely, that teaching is about giving students an opportunity to learn, but that this involves many different things on the teacher's part; things described and explained above.

The purpose of the chapter has not just been to introduce you to these different aspects, but to encourage you to reflect on your own experiences, assumptions and beliefs. And to consider how these might change and develop as your training progresses.

We will finish with a few questions on which you might like to reflect, as well as a few short activities you can undertake to further interrogate your existing understanding of teaching.

Questions for Reflection

- What does teaching mean to you? Do you agree with the different answers I have set out? Would you add anything or take anything away?

- Can teaching get in the way of learning? Why?

- To what extent has your own schooling shaped your attitude to teaching and learning?

- Does a teacher have to be memorable to be good? Why?

Activities

- Make a list of the teachers who have had the biggest impact on you throughout your education. For each one, identify why they had an impact and what you can take away from this to inform your own practice.

- Rank the different answers I have given to the question from most to least importance. Add in any other answers of your own you think I have missed. Then, consider why you have ranked them this way and what this might mean for your teaching style.

- Challenge yourself to re-order the answers in a manner with which you don't agree. Try to develop a coherent argument explaining why someone else might opt for this ranking. Then, reflect on your original choices and assess whether you still stand by them.

Chapter Two – What Is Learning All About?

Having gone some way towards unpacking the idea of teaching, we turn now to learning.

The aim here is similar; to answer the question 'What is learning all about?' by providing a series of answers, each possessing its own merit and each asking you to look at the concept from a slightly different perspective.

Our purpose echoes that underpinning the previous chapter.

First, we are seeking to develop a more nuanced, analytical understanding of what learning is. Second, we are positing the idea that the question does not have a definitive answer; rather, a set of possible answers, all of which reveal certain truths. Third, and arising from these two points, that becoming an outstanding trainee teacher involves, in part, thinking critically about learning; both the learning of which we have experience and the learning we seek to facilitate for our students.

A General Answer

In general, learning is all about development. The development of our capacities, of our knowledge, of our understanding. If learning has taken place, we should be more than we were prior to its happening. If we are not, it is hard to say convincingly that learning really has occurred.

Dredge your memory in search of a bad learning experience from your past. Perhaps it occurred at school, at university or while you were learning to drive.

Why was the experience bad? What caused it to fail? Why did you not learn much from it, if anything, and how did that leave you feeling as a result?

Chances are that the memory evokes at least some sense of frustration or wastefulness. You gave some of your time (willingly or not) and you knew that the intention behind the process was for you to learn. Yet you didn't. You left the session or the lesson little changed from when you entered it.

This illustrates the general idea that learning provokes change and that this change is the central aim of all learning. The change is rarely profound or significant. It invariably involves us knowing a little bit more, understanding a little better or being able to act in a manner which is slightly more skilful.

And this is another part of our general answer. Learning is a cumulative process. It takes time, effort and repetition. Or, to put it another way, practice.

While any learning experience will be predicated on a concept of growth, change or development, the wider experience of learning – over a series of lessons, or a course of study – marks a more tangible experience of these processes than is generally possible within a single instance.

Let us take learning to drive as an example. In a single driving lesson, we will probably notice ourselves getting a bit better. At the end, it is likely that, if we were asked to reflect, we would be able to identify the change in our abilities.

However, if we were to reflect on the growth of our skills, knowledge and understanding over the course of twenty driving lessons (if, indeed, we needed this many!), the situation would be rather different.

Our development would be much clearer, much greater and much more significant.

In many ways this seems a banal point, but it is worth dwelling on for two reasons.

First, as we noted in the previous chapter, the unit through which teachers work is the lesson. And this is generally a fairly brief period of time. Therefore, students are likely to struggle to identify the learning and progress they make unless we give them a helping hand in this matter.

Second, cumulative gains as a direct function of practice and effort are the driving force of learning over time. If you don't have experience or awareness of this (and sometimes, even if you do), making the requisite leap of faith required to persistently strive and drive yourself forwards can be a challenge.

Hence why it is incumbent upon the teacher to support all students in doing this.

Knowledge

Perhaps the most straightforward way in which learning can be identified is in terms of knowledge. If we know more than was previously was the case, we have learned. Simple.

A student enters a lesson, time passes, and they come out knowing more about the topic than they did when they entered. Learning has thus taken place.

But what is knowledge, exactly? And is it possible to accurately measure an individual's possession of it?

Well, philosophers have long argued over the status of knowledge (the branch of the discipline dealing with the issue is called epistemology) and we do not have the space here to digress any distance into these debates.

Instead, let me offer a more classroom-focussed analysis, based on my experiences of teaching and learning.

Knowledge, I would argue, consists simply of the pieces of information we want students to know about any given topic. This extends to, but is not restricted to, the following: facts, concepts, words, symbols, definitions and meanings. It is a brief list, not definitive, but designed to exemplify the point.

Put another way, knowledge is the content of the curriculum in its most basic form. The blocks from which the curriculum is constructed, minus the elements of understanding and skills to which we attend below.

Thought of like this, knowledge connects closely to the idea of remembering, whereby students are asked to memorise the information presented to them and the teacher confirms memorisation through testing – usually in the form of recall.

This aspect of learning is vitally important, but partial nonetheless.

It is important because, in order to know about a topic, you must be able to remember the important pieces of information related to that topic. Similarly, you must be able to communicate about that topic in an effective manner – using the appropriate words and so forth – not only to demonstrate the knowledge which has been learned, but also to reinforce, refine and develop that knowledge (with this taking place through the articulation of thoughts and the cognitive work which precedes and follows articulation).

It is partial because, to know something does not mean by necessity that you understand something. I could memorise a series of equations to do with civil engineering, but it would not mean I understood those equations. I may do, or I may not. Either way, the understanding is not a direct function of the knowing.

With that said, understanding cannot come without some level of knowledge, suggesting that the latter is a prerequisite for the former, even if its influence on whether or not the former will develop is by no means certain.

To further illustrate the fact that knowledge and understanding are bound up with each other, consider the fact that rote learning is useful in some situations (as when, for example, students simply have to know the meaning of a word or the result of an equation) but falls short of being a generally effective learning method. This is because it asks only that something is remembered – not that it can be applied, analysed or evaluated. To do any of that, a degree of understanding is required. And this can only be achieved through methods which go beyond the limited efficacy of rote learning.

Understanding

So perhaps learning is actually all about understanding. Understanding involves more than just knowing. It takes us into the realm of more complex cognitive processes. These include application, analysis and evaluation, as mentioned above, as well as explanation, comparison, critique and variations on these themes.

But let us try to broaden things out for a moment, such that we might say, in general, what understanding is.

Understanding means we can explain and use ideas, information and facts. It means we know how to do things, as well as know things in and of themselves. For me, it is with the idea of 'use' that understanding gains real traction.

As noted above, knowing something does not by itself confer the ability to do anything with that which we know, other than to recall it. This indicates how memorisation has as its end the ability to bring to mind that which was memorised, not necessarily to do anything other with the thing in question.

For example, a child might rote learn their six times table. This is good and important. We ask them to recall the table for us and they do so, with complete accuracy. But the utility of this learning only really comes about when we move forward and the child begins to use their knowledge to do things. It is in this doing that the child comes to develop an understanding of number beyond the bare facts of recall.

They might come to see links between different sums; be able to apply their knowledge of the six times table in various calculations; or identify patterns and relationships between figures, shapes and so forth.

This illustrates both the limitations and importance of knowing things off-by-heart. The knowing is not sufficient in itself, but it is necessary and vital for giving students a sound basis from which to develop understanding.

Returning to our suggestion that understanding connects to being able to use the things we know, this idea can be further supported by looking at the understanding experts possess.

When we see an expert at work – whether this involves a purely intellectual activity such as debating or an activity of another type such as glass-blowing – what is clear is the expert's ability to use their knowledge with great skill and precision. To the extent that what might be highly complex can often appear simple or easy...until you try it yourself!

This points to the fact that understanding is best thought of as a continuum, ranging from an origin at which no understanding is possessed to a far-off point of complete mastery.

Thinking in this way further highlights the contrast between knowing and understanding. We can know things, know more things or even know all there is to know about highly specific things. However, in all these instances it remains the case that our knowledge is essentially tied up with knowing – possessing bits of information.

Understanding, on the other hand, seems to exist in more dimensions. We can come to understand something more deeply; we can understand things in greater depth, in more detail or with enhanced clarity. And a new perspective can cause us to see what we thought we knew in a different light (a changed light having a much greater effect if the thing being lit is three-dimensional).

So knowledge and understanding are bound together, the latter being based, at least in part, on use of the former, with that use flowing along a continuum of mastery.

Skills

A different answer to the question 'What is learning all about?' is the word 'skills.'

Often, in education, content and skills are set against each other. The opposition, it is argued, comes from the fact that the former is all about learning information while the latter deals with practising and developing abilities.

As with knowledge and understanding, skills cannot reasonably sit as a separate and distinct entity. When we talk about learning skills, we must be mindful to remember that skills exist and are used within a context – always. It can never be the case that skills exist independently of all else. This is logically impossible.

Possessing a skill; learning a skill. Both these statements imply that the general form (skills) is made concrete in something particular (the skill of critical thinking or the skill of being able to think through the consequences of a design idea). And, in being made concrete, it is immediately tied up with the real world – as well as the knowledge and understanding we possess.

For example, in a Citizenship lesson we might be helping students to learn about the skill of debating. We begin with some general thoughts and discussion, but soon lead into application of the skill to concrete scenarios.

We might ask students to debate a certain topic, to critique an argument about a given issue or to write a peroration for a speech covering a recent area of study.

This application of skills – practice in process, as it were – suggests that, while it is possible to speak of skills in an abstract sense, even to learn about them through the use of general exercises or examples, such work will be inherently limited.

For skills-based learning to be effective – for it to be meaningful and useful – it must be grounded in knowledge and understanding.

It is here that we come to a realisation about the nature of learning in the classroom which I'm sure you have already grasped. While we can talk about aspects of that learning as if they are separate – knowledge, understanding and skills – the reality is that this is rarely, if ever, the case. All three are bound up together; and usually inseparable in most good lessons.

With that said, it has been helpful for us to attend to each element in turn. Doing so gives us an opportunity to think about how learning as a whole might work in our classrooms. It also allows us to consider how the balance between the three areas can alter, depending on the type of lesson we are teaching and the stage our students are at.

Conceptual Understanding

An area of thought some would argue is the answer to our question about the nature of learning is conceptual understanding.

Concepts are ideas. They are abstractions which refer to intangible things. Courage is a concept. It does not exist in the world in the same way as a lump of rock. Instead of being an object, it is an idea. We can witness someone being courageous, but we cannot go into a shop and pick up a piece of courage. (For more on this dilemma, see The Wizard of Oz!)

Concepts are the foundation of much of our thought. It could be argued that they are the intellectual embodiment of culture, with culture being the way of life (mental as well as experiential) which people within a society share.

Consider, for example, how young children have to learn even the most basic concepts. Concepts which we as adults take for granted. Such as time, sharing or truth. Then consider how, as children grow older, their conceptual understanding develops.

A five year-old conceives of time differently to a fifteen year-old, even if they can both use the concept in speech. Similarly, a five year-old may talk about sharing in a very basic sense, whereas a twenty-five year-old may talk about sharing through a political lens, using the concept as the basis for an argument about redistribution of wealth and the provision of public goods.

Here we can see how we continue to rely on concepts throughout our lives. Without any understanding of them we would not be able to think or communicate as we can. We would probably not even conceive of ourselves as people. The term 'person' is a concept, after all.

Learning then, is primarily about the development of conceptual understanding. This development includes a growing sense of depth and nuance regarding the meaning and use of concepts – but so too does it entail broadening the mental maps upon which our concepts sit.

So, for example, learning knowledge in the form of facts and information gives us a more detailed vista of thought from which we can engage with concepts; helping us to develop our conceptual understanding just as much as does the process of interrogating, analysing and applying concepts.

Another way to think about the development of conceptual understanding is that, through learning, we become wiser. That wisdom is a result of us knowing more and being able to do more. As this process occurs, we find ourselves moving closer to the reality of things; a reality which is too vast to ever be fully comprehended, but which we can come to know better as we continue to learn.

The only problem with moving down this wisdom route is that the term is notoriously tricky to define. To that end, it may not serve our purpose here.

Nonetheless, seeing learning as, at least to some degree, the development of conceptual understanding, means thinking about what we do in the classroom as having a direct impact on the maps of the world students use to try to navigate society, culture and their own experiences. I think this is a nice metaphor, because it allows us to envisage learning (and teaching) as being concerned with adding detail, depth and breadth to those maps, as well as helping students to use them ever more accurately, critically and carefully.

Processes

We move now to a rather more instrumental answer to the question. Here we can argue that learning is all about processes. By this we mean the processes we use in order to learn.

Such an answer serves to draw our attention to the fact that learning is itself a process. This is because it involves the learner doing a series of things which (hopefully) lead to a desired end.

For example, a student may spend time practising a dance move with the aim of perfecting it. As they do this, they note the improvements which come from correcting small errors, as well as the increased familiarity they gain through repetition. Whether the student is consciously aware of this process or not is an interesting point. They do not need to be in order to use it to good effect, but they may well be able to use it more effectively if they are.

Here we come on to a commonly argued theme concerning learning. Expert learners tend to be actively engaged with the process of their own learning.

An expert artist experimenting with a new medium, for instance, will likely direct a good deal of their mental energy toward analysing and evaluating the results of what they do, before using this information to make changes and adaptations. A less expert artist might use the medium, then step back and think about what happened. A still-less expert artist may use the medium and then wonder why things didn't turn out as they hoped.

Certain elements of the learning process are universal, other aspects differ according to what you are learning and how you are learning it.

The use of memory is one universal process – something on which all learning depends. Consider, if you will, the sad story of a man with amnesia who has to learn his name again every morning when he wakes up. His case points to the centrality of memory while also implying that an active engagement with memory – through the use of aides or mnemonics, for example – can help us to marshal the forces at our disposal more effectively.

Another universal process is trial and error. Again, the efficacy of its deployment tends to vary depending on whether it is done consciously, semi-consciously or without any thought at all.

We often see trial and error at its freest and least constrained in very young children. They constantly explore, test and experiment with their surroundings, usually with no concern as to whether they have made a mistake or not. It is only later that fear of failure begins to rear its head, as we grow older and the scope of our world changes.

But consider also the essential playfulness of many creative individuals – artists, musicians, scientists, inventors. Here we have often much older people who retain (or have cultivated) a child-like sense of engagement with trial and error. Who, crucially, see it as a useful process, rather than as a threat.

This all helps draw us back to the central conceit that learning is all about processes. In so doing, it gives us food for thought in terms of how we might help our students to think about their learning – and how we might think about our own as well.

Failure and Success

Which leads us nicely to the topics of failure and success.

Learning, surely, must be about these, mustn't it?

I mean, when you learn, you either succeed or fail don't you? If you can do more than you could previously, if you know more than you did before the learning began, then you have succeeded. If you don't, or you can't, you've failed.

Is it really as simple as that?

Well, yes and no.

First, we have the undoubted fact that learning can be viewed in terms of success and failure. The point of reference will usually be whether the ends we set out to achieve have been reached. If they have, success is ours, if they haven't, we are faced failure.

Second, when it comes to learning in a classroom context, whether we have succeeded or failed is usually pretty easy to judge – particularly if we have a method of assessment such as a test, question or exam paper on hand to give us an accurate summary.

On the other hand, though, failure and success seem like somewhat ham-fisted concepts when applied in this way. They give rise to the idea of learning as a zero-sum game. You either win or lose; and that's the end of it.

A better approach might see us redefining the concepts, such that their application starts to have different effects.

Beginning with success, we need to ask what success actually looks like – both from the perspective of the learner and from that of the teacher. When thought of in this way, success starts to become less like a monolith which we can either climb or not, and more like a series of steps – some of which will be harder to climb than others, but all of which are potentially in reach.

One of the reasons learners can see success in a dualistic sense (total or non-existent) is because their understanding of what they are setting out to learn is, naturally, limited. This couples with their often restricted experience of the process of learning, making it difficult for them to look at a large, far-off goal (being able to do what they want to be able to do) and break this down into smaller, more manageable sections.

So learning is about success, but that success needs to be redefined. Learners are often unable to do this and the teacher needs to step in and do it on their behalf.

A similar story can be told about failure. Again, learners often see it as an absolute, as opposed to something which can be taken apart and which possesses nuance.

No failure connected to learning in the classroom is absolute; and every failure presents us with information we can use to develop and make progress. Here, the difficulty comes in having to change the perceptions students might hold about what failure means. The process of re-education, or challenging their preconceptions, is an important part of the teacher's work. As you will note, it links closely to what we have said already about the development of conceptual understanding and the importance of process.

Agency

We now tack far away from our previous answers and look at a somewhat deeper and more personal angle on what learning is.

Agency, in a sociological and philosophical sense, is the ability of an individual to act in the world. A prisoner has much of their agency removed, as does someone who is oppressed.

When it comes to learning, the whole process is very much about promoting, enlarging and bestowing agency. Or, to put it another way, increasing and improving a student's ability to act in the world.

Literacy is the keenest example of this. While a person who cannot read or write may well be successful and live a life which is good, they will also find themselves cut off from accessing a significant portion of human experience. Even more, they will find acting in the world difficult in certain situations, not least because of the central role the written word plays in society and culture.

Imagine now that this individual, in later life, after they have passed through formal schooling, learns how to read and write. This would represent a major change in their life. One which would bring them a far greater degree of agency than was previously the case. As their literacy skills improve, so too will their ability to act in the world; their agency.

We can draw the point more widely by saying that learning allows us to become more than we were, and that with each step we take through such a process, the wealth of possibilities open to us grows a little larger.

These possibilities may be physical or mental, external or internal. Examples include the opportunity to access jobs of certain types and the opportunity to think about our experiences and emotions in a way which is more accurate and precise. Both examples see learning as being about increasing our capacities to be human, to be successful, to be known and understood; to be who we are, or who we want to be.

There is a risk that this might be dismissed as too vague, too unfocussed. But to see learning in purely utilitarian terms is to miss the fundamental difference there is between knowing and not knowing, being able to and not being able to. That difference amounts to a small gap in many places, but a huge chasm in others.

Learning nearly always contributes to an individual's agency – extending the boundaries of how they can act in the world. Sometimes it makes a small change; sometimes an enormous one. Regardless, however, of what learning takes place, a change of some sort will always occur.

This vision of learning – and it is a vision – as a transformative experience tied to a human being's capacity to act in the world, their agency, is easily lost in the necessarily formalised and bureaucratic land of centrally-funded and centrally-administered education. But it is worth holding onto. If only to remind us of the deeply humane aspect of the job we as teachers are setting out to do.

Personal Fulfilment

Abraham Maslow, a twentieth century psychologist with whom you may be familiar, produced a hierarchy of needs as part of his work. This hierarchy, Maslow argued, represents those things which human beings need, ordered according to the relative necessity of those needs. Hence, we find physiological and safety needs at the bottom. Breathing, food, water, shelter, protection and so on being the foundation on which other needs rest.

Above these we find Maslow's third category: love and belonging, in which he placed friendship, family and sexual intimacy. The fourth category is esteem, including the respect of others, confidence and a sense of achievement. Finally, at the top of the pyramid, is self-actualisation. This includes needs Maslow identified as being central to fulfilling your personal potential – to becoming who or what you feel you can be.

There is much debate around whether Maslow's hierarchy ought to be accepted. And, indeed, it has been considerably developed since the construction of the initial model which I have outlined.

We do not need to go into the debates here, however. Rather, we can use the hierarchy to help us think about learning's role in personal fulfilment. And, by extension, the wider pleasure which can be derived from learning, as well as the important role it plays in many people's lives.

It is not by mistake that the phrase 'learning for learning's sake' exists. It indicates the fact that learning is not just a means to an end but can also be an end in itself. Learning about a topic for no other reason than that you find it interesting is as good a reason as any to pursue a course of study, however informal this may be.

Personal fulfilment is seen as a desirable goal in many societies. It is frequently tied up with a person's attempt to fulfil their potential – to push themselves to grow, change and become more than they are.

And what is this if not a description of learning?

Children, though, are compelled to go to school. Of course, it is absolutely right that this is so...but they may not always see it like that! This leads us to a position whereby learning can, for them, take on a perfunctory meaning somewhat removed from the rewarding sense of personal fulfilment about which we are thinking here.

Finding ways to make this aspect of learning a reality in an old, familiar classroom is a task for all teachers. Those who succeed in meeting it usually draw a memorable response from their students.

Acculturation

And so we come to our final answer to the question of what learning is. And it directly mirrors the final answer we gave in the previous chapter, when we looked at teaching. I include it here in order to draw the circle to a close, reminding us that teaching and learning, while separate, are dependent on each other and, always, closely intertwined.

It is through learning that children and young adults come to be full members of the culture or society to which they belong. This process helps them to make the transition from being completely dependent on the family unit to being able to, however tentatively, and perhaps only partly, stand on their own feet, independent and ready to fend for themselves.

As Marshall McLuhan noted some years ago, the medium is the message. While he was talking about the media, we can apply his insight to education. The entire process of formal schooling through which students pass – a process which now involves you in your role as a teacher-in-the-making – is itself a message about what society is and what culture consists of.

That message rests in part on the charge, sometimes implicit, often explicit, that education is vitally important. The medium tells us this. Over a decade of compulsory schooling signifies quite clearly that learning matters.

It also rests on what happens during those years of schooling. It is for this reason, among others, that the relative inconsistency of school experience across a country is frequently held up as a problem. The argument is not that all schooling should be identical. Rather, that it ought to meet similar standards, if we want to send the message to our country's children that all have the opportunity to succeed and that all are deemed equally worthy of input and support from the state (which in a democracy, let us not forget, is, or ought to be, a manifestation of the will of the people, paid for out of the people's pockets).

Learning then, is as much about acculturation and socialisation as anything else. And the medium through which it is experienced is as powerful as anything else in terms of the concomitant messages it conveys.

So let us not forget that you, as a teacher, have a great deal of control over the medium of your teaching. Maybe not the medium of your school, or the system at large. But certainly over your teaching.

Thinking about that will stand you in good stead when you decide what type of messages you want your lessons, your interactions, your communication and all the rest of it to convey.

We will leave things there. What learning is now seems both clearer and more obscure – a mark of the fact that we have opened up a series of answers to the question, but in so doing also intimated the unlikelihood that a definitive answer can be settled upon.

As with the previous chapter, the aim has been to provoke a critical, nuanced engagement with an old, familiar idea.

This will help you to reflect on your own experiences with greater rigour and detachment. It will also provide you with a way to think about your students' learning which is both analytical and searching.

Such an approach should help you to make excellent progress in this, your first year in the profession.

We conclude with some questions and activities you can use to reflect further on the nature of learning.

Questions

- What have been your best learning experiences? Why were they good?

- How can a teacher get in the way of learning? How can they facilitate learning which might otherwise be difficult to achieve? If possible, call on your own experiences when thinking about these questions.

- Is all learning equal? Why?

- What do you think about when you are learning? How does this affect the learning you do?

- How do you know when you have learned something? And how do you know when you have mastered something?

Activities

- Make a table containing five of your best learning experiences and five of your worst. Compare the lists. Ask yourself why they differ. What can you take away from this analysis to use in your own teaching?

- Interview three friends or family members. Ask them about their experiences of learning, what they think learning is and how they view the process. Compare their answers to your own reflections and see what conclusions you can draw.

- Observe an experienced teacher with a reputation for being very good at their job. Examine the role learning plays in their lesson. What do students do? How does the teacher manage learning? What is the focus of the lesson? What language is used? If possible, talk to students and the teacher about these questions as well; then compare their responses with your observation notes.

Chapter Three – Becoming a Teacher

In Chapters One and Two we sought to develop a critical understanding of the central elements of a teacher's job – teaching and learning. In this chapter our focus moves to some of the practical things about which all teachers need to know. The aim is to give you an insight, at this early stage, into the most important aspects of day-to-day life as a trainee teacher, other than teaching and learning.

In the chapters which follow we will return to teaching and learning, exploring them in significant detail.

For now, let us think about practical matters – both general and specific.

Practical Matters

Schools are fantastic places to work. They vary greatly and one of the challenges facing a trainee teacher is deciding what type of school they would like to work in. I will leave that challenge to you, though, as here my intention is to give a crash course in some of the practical matters – both large and small – which come with working in a school.

First we have geography. You need to be able to find your way around. This can be more complex than it sounds. Some schools are labyrinthine in structure, often as a result of historical building works which have been undertaken periodically, leading to a structure lacking coherent planning.

On beginning your training, whether this involves a short placement of a few months or an extended stay, you should spend a little while finding your way around. This will make your life much easier further down the road. Don't be afraid to roam the corridors if you have a free lesson. Wandering round will help you to get your bearings. If you fear being pulled up for not working, carry a piece of paper with you – it is a sure-fire method for making it look like there is a deeper purpose to your wanderings!

Identify key sections of the school: departments or year groups; toilets; reception; offices; staff room; photocopiers; entrances and exits. If the option is available, ask someone to give you a tour – this could be students as well as staff.

Having assessed the lay of the land, make sure you quickly find out where resources are kept, how photocopying is accessed and how to log on to the computer system. This is all basic stuff with which I'm sure you will be familiar. I mention it here as much out of a sense of completeness as anything else.

Next is familiarising yourself with the school day. This is vital, not least so you can ensure you are forever punctual and have a clear understanding of how much time is available in between the various things you are expected to do or attend.

Rules are next – those covering students and those covering staff. The former include the school's behaviour policy. Or, what to do if things go wrong! Having a sound understanding of the school rules will make life in the classroom much easier. Students will soon work out whether you know your stuff or not.

Rules for staff are usually fairly brief and often cover basics such as dress code, expected attendance at meetings, car parking and such like. Getting a swift grasp on these will ensure you meet them and don't end up in an embarrassing situation in which someone has to direct you as to the appropriate way to act.

Unwritten rules are important as well. For example, do students and staff maintain generally formal or informal greetings, are briefings held in the staff room on a Monday, and is it seen as bad form to 'cc' line managers into non-urgent emails? The aim here is to think about the norms which underpin social interaction in the school. Picking up on these and working in conjunction with them will make people positively disposed towards you (which, in turn, will deliver the general benefit of making your training more enjoyable).

Other practical matters to consider include familiarising yourself with the school's software (what do they use to take the register? Is there a virtual learning environment?), procedures for getting in and out of the building, when the building opens and closes, as well as any relevant information about the local area.

The wider point here is that, when embarking on your training, you will be entering a fully functioning institution filled with people, rules, norms and systems. Getting on top of all this as soon as possible will make your life easier, and allow you to focus on your teaching and the learning your students do.

The Curriculum

The curriculum is our next port of call, neatly combining the practical with the pedagogical.

You will be expected to teach lessons which tally with the curriculum your training school is already using. In some cases this will be set directly by the government, in others by an exam board, and in others it will have been decided internally – by a department or year group team – usually in partial conjunction with aims or guidelines provided by the government or the school's leadership team.

Familiarising yourself with the curriculum you will be expected to teach – or curricula depending on your areas of expertise – is essential. While some trainee teachers opt for the wait and see approach, this is a difficult path from which to become outstanding.

A better option is to find out which curriculum is being used and to get hold of a copy. You can then spend time looking through this, allowing you to build up a picture of what it contains, to understand the rationale behind its construction and to assess what existing knowledge you have and what additional information you might need to seek out.

Curricula provided by the government are available online. These vary in the extent of their prescription. Some schools also carry printed copies, although this is increasingly rare. Exam board curricula are also available via the internet. These are usually referred to as specifications, meaning the specification of what an examined course of study ought to cover.

The main exam boards at the time of writing are AQA, OCR and Edexcel. If you are training to teach secondary age children, you should find out which exam boards your department uses so as to ensure you research the correct specifications.

Beyond this, most schools will have administrative documents mapping the programmes of study (a term almost synonymous with curriculum) students are expected follow at different ages and/or in different subjects. You should ask your mentor where these are kept and read through them to get a sense of what teaching and learning in your subject or year group is based upon.

If you have multiple school placements during your training period, be sure to repeat the process – there will always be differences between what one school does and what another opts for. Being alive to this and researching it in advance will help you to avoid any nasty surprises.

The final place in which you can look to find information about the curriculum is the existing lessons teachers in your department or year group have planned. With any luck, these will be available through a shared folder on the school's computer network. If they are, great! You can browse through them at leisure. This will help you to get a sense of what the curriculum is, as well as what the content looks like when translated into lesson form.

If lessons are not freely available, you will need to ask colleagues if they are happy to give you access. Explain why you want to look at them and this is unlikely to be a problem.

When seeking to be an outstanding trainee teacher, familiarity with the curriculum is an important point to address. The better you understand what you are being asked to teach, the better placed you will be to create outstanding lessons.

In addition, if you have a good understanding of what the curriculum as a whole looks like, and the reasons behind its design, you will be better placed to plan learning for students and to talk to them about where you and they are going, as well as why you are going there.

As a final note, you might find it instructive to research the wider history of the curriculum. This can be done quickly and easily on the internet. While this research will not have a direct bearing on what you do in the classroom, it will help to contextualise the present situation for you, giving you a better understanding of the political and pedagogical drivers underpinning the current way of doing things.

Roles

A multitude of roles exist within any school. Some of these are common across many institutions, some are unique to a single school. To get a sense of how names for fairly standard roles (teacher, head of department, assistant head teacher) can proliferate into a wide range of nomenclature, take a look through the jobs being advertised on the TES website (www.tes.co.uk/jobs). There you will find learning coaches, team leaders, change activators and much else besides.

It will serve your cause well to become au fait with the different roles in you school. This will help you to discern how accountability is distributed in the institution, who is responsible for what, and who to call on should you need support with a particular matter.

Here I will give a brief overview of the key roles you are likely to come across.

The **headteacher** or **principal** is in charge of the school. Generally, they will have been a practising teacher themselves and will have worked their way up the management structure. Some schools have an **executive headteacher** or **executive principal**. Such a person looks after a number of schools, offering leadership to each while second-in-commands deal with the day-to-day running of the schools in question.

The **senior leadership team** (commonly referred to as the **SLT**) are a group of teachers, all of whom have senior managerial responsibilities and who work with the headteacher to run the school. **Deputy headteachers** or **vice principals** are second in charge. There are usually between 1 and 3 of these roles in a school. **Assistant headteachers** or **assistant principals** are found on the next rung of the management ladder. These roles tend to come with specific areas of whole-school responsibility. Numbers can vary from 2 – 10 depending on the size and budget of the school.

Following this we have **middle management.** These are teachers who have been given managerial responsibility below that of the senior leadership team. In a secondary school this includes **heads of departments** and pastoral leaders such as **heads of house** or **heads of year.** In primary schools, responsibilities are often conferred to cover subject specialisms and year groups.

Outside these roles you will usually find **administrative staff**, a **bursar** or **director of finance, receptionists, caretakers** and **reprographics staff.**

Everybody in school has an important role to play. If you want to do well, be pleasant, friendly and positive. An obvious point, sure. But never underestimate the power of reputation. Even if you have a short placement, people will quickly make up their minds about you – whether their opinions are accurate or not! And this information is likely to be brought up in the kind of run-of-the-mill conversations people have on a daily basis.

Now, while it is unlikely that anything here could work against you, consider how a glowing recommendation, or even a kind word, can work in your favour if heard by your mentor or a member of SLT (who may be looking to recruit trainee teachers into full-time posts).

From my own experience, I would strongly recommend developing a good relationship with whoever is in charge of the photocopier – if they like you, they may well save your bacon if an unexpected need for immediate pre-lesson copying ever arises!

Two final points regarding roles before we move on.

Understanding who is responsible for what means you are in a position to ask the right person for the right help as and when it is required. It also makes it easier for you to use the school's systems effectively.

As a trainee teacher, you will encounter a number of roles which are relevant only to you and your fellow trainees. Your mentor, of course. But also quite likely a coordinator of the professional studies programme; called a PCM in some schools.

Developing a positive relationship with the holders of these roles is vital if you want to be outstanding.

They are the key people responsible for monitoring your progress and for observing your teaching. Try to gauge their characters early and then mould yourself to fit; giving them information in a way which suits how they think, for example.

Other than this, the best advice when it comes to working with your mentor and PCM (or equivalent) is that almost everybody values and respects punctuality, good organisation, hard work, a positive attitude and the ability to learn from constructive criticism.

The Training Process

Next we turn to the training process, about which I will say only a few things, though each one is important in its own right.

First is timing. A good understanding of the timing of those events which form part of your training is necessary if you want to be outstanding. You should identify what is expected of you at what point and, in the process, pick out any potential pinch points. For example, do you have to hand an assignment in the same week that your teaching load increases? Or is an important assessment point scheduled for the same week as a friend's wedding?

Knowing how your course pans out means you can deal with potential trouble spots in advance. It will help you to understand where you are going, giving you a precise roadmap to which you can return when things get busy during the course of the year. And it will allow you to see the course from the viewpoint of others. This can provide perspective. It can also help you to work in such a way that you make life easy for your tutor and mentor – something that will not go unnoticed.

Armed with an understanding of timing, you will be in a position to plan ahead. Doing so will give you a chance to stagger your workload. This will not make training a complete doddle. Inevitably there will be periods when you have a lot of work on. But it will allow you to think about how to prevent an excessive workload developing.

For example, you might note that there is a quiet period before the Christmas holidays (I said might!) and decide to use this as an opportunity to get an assignment ticked off or to work on your portfolio. Whatever decisions you take, they will be better for having been made in advance, with a clear understanding of what is likely to be expected and on what deadline.

Finally, we come to the requirements your course makes for a trainee to be deemed outstanding. In the last chapter, when we looked at the nature of learning, one of the answers I suggested was that learning is essentially a matter of success and failure. On unpacking this, we saw how success is easier to achieve if the criteria by which that success is judged are made accessible to learners. In the classroom, that is part of the teacher's job.

Outside the classroom, we need to be independent and take this job on for ourselves.

If you want to be an outstanding trainee teacher – and I am sure that you do – then your mission will be made a lot simpler if you know what you need to do to achieve this. The convenor of your course will likely have provided you with documents indicating what is necessary for an outstanding grading.

Read through these. Think about what they mean. Talk to your mentor about them. Take advantage of their experience. Ask them to contextualise the criteria by giving you concrete examples.

If anything feels vague or ambiguous, ask for clarification. Collect any queries you have and share them with the person running your course (this is a better approach than firing off emails as and when you think of something, which can be annoying for the person on the other end).

And why not ask for examples of previous assignments which scored highly? Or to look at previous portfolios of trainee teachers who were graded outstanding? Or find a member of staff in your school who can show you what an outstanding lesson looks like. You could even take your observation matrix into the lesson with you and tick off what they do as and when they do it.

The aim here is to give yourself the best chance of being successful – to set yourself up for success. With a little thought, planning and analysis, this is easy to achieve. Following the steps above will give you a precise idea of what is needed to be graded outstanding, making it much easier to achieve the mark.

Working with Children and Young Adults

We move now to the crux of what you will be doing as a trainee teacher: learning to work effectively with children and/or young adults. The age group with whom you work will be determined by your decision to train as a primary school teacher or a secondary school teacher.

The first thing to be aware of is that we all bring a series of assumptions and preconceptions to our training, with these predisposing us to view children and young adults in a certain light.

For example, you may retain an idealised view of the teacher's role. Through rose-tinted glasses you will imagine that with a little bit of creativity and ingenuity, any child can be won over to the joys of learning and hard work. Alternatively, you may have a perception that only some children are capable of paying attention for extended periods, and that you will need to do lots of things to support those for whom this is impossible.

Assumptions and preconceptions are often false. If they do ever turn out to be true (and those above do not), this validation only occurs by comparing them to evidence. That evidence comes through experience.

Two points follow.

First, you should spend some time reflecting on your own assumptions and on the preconceptions with which you are entering your training. This is not easy. You will need to be critical and objective, viewing your own thinking with a sense of detachment. The task is worthwhile, however, as it will give you an insight into how you are thinking, prior to actually working in the role of classroom teacher.

Second, you should question any assumptions or preconceptions you identify. They might be correct or they might be wrong. You will need to test them against the reality of teaching. If they prove incorrect, be prepared to let them go.

Failing to engage in this process makes becoming an outstanding trainee teacher more difficult. This is because you will find yourself in situations which feel dispiriting or off-putting. Having the assumptions through which you think challenged can be a difficult experience. This is compounded if the experience is unexpected – or if it happens and you do not have a conscious understanding of what, exactly, is happening.

Let me give you an example.

Imagine we enter our training assuming that all children want to learn and look forward to coming into school. This assumption then informs our thinking and, crucially, our expectations.

When our expectations are not met, we feel uncomfortable and frustrated. And if we are not consciously aware of the role the assumption is playing in our thinking, we may struggle to understand why this is the case.

Often, the consequence of such events is that relationships between teacher and students can become strained, or less positive than we would like them to be.

Now imagine we identified the assumption prior to starting our training. We would not necessarily reject it, but we would be in a position to question it and to wait and see whether or not the experience of being in the classroom offered confirmation or refutation.

Operating from this position, we are less likely to become uncomfortable or frustrated. This is because our expectations have been tempered by an acceptance that our beliefs, prior to being tested in the arena of the classroom, may not be accurate.

In conclusion, managing your own expectations of what the job entails and what it is like to work with children and/or young adults will help you to avoid negative emotions. It also makes your more alive to the information your experiences provide, helping you to avoid hanging onto ways of thinking which run counter to these experiences.

Of course, I am not advocating a rejection of ideals! Rather, an acknowledgement that they are just that – ideals – and will not necessarily be reflected by the reality you encounter. (If they aren't, how you bridge that gap becomes the next question you need to answer.)

The second thing we must consider when working with children and young adults is that they are passing through an extended period of development. This encompasses physical, emotional, social, intellectual and psychological development.

Not only is the period of formal schooling a period in which students develop their understanding of thought and the world as defined by the curriculum, but so too is it a period in which many more developmental changes occur.

From here, we can note that, to be an outstanding trainee teacher, it is well worth becoming acquainted with the developmental journeys students go through. You should tailor your investigations to the age groups with whom you are working.

So, for example, if you are training to teach at secondary level, you will place yourself in a strong position if you gain a basic understanding of the changes the brain goes through during the teenage years, as well as the role of hormones in shaping and influencing behaviour. Similarly, if you are training to teach much younger children, becoming expert in the psychology of child development, including the development of cognition and the stages through which all children are expected to pass, will be of great benefit.

Being able to interpret some of the behaviour and thinking in which students engage will help you to make better decisions. The simple fact of being able to explain – even if your explanation is only partial – why certain things are happening, places you in a better position than if you have no clue.

Working with Colleagues

As well as working with students, you will also work with colleagues. Here there are few things we must say.

First, colleagues are a source of information and experience. Asking for support, help and advice allows you to tap into this. While teachers are generally fairly busy people, gilding any request for support with a reference to the status of the individual in question should help matters run smoothly. Compare these two requests as evidence of this fact:

A) Can you tell me what you think about this lesson?

B) In your experience, do you think this is a good way to engage students?

The second statement represents a subtle recasting of the question. The aim is not to mislead, but simply to oil the wheels of social interaction in a busy environment.

Earlier, we explored some of the roles which exist in school and considered their relative importance. Understanding what colleagues do makes your life easier. Primarily, this is because you then know who to go to for different matters. This improves the likelihood of receiving the information or support you want and also makes you look professional.

If you are not sure who is responsible for a given area, or if you want to know who is the best person to speak to about a certain topic, ask your mentor.

One of the best ways to quickly develop your understanding of teaching and learning in a classroom context is to observe colleagues teach. Aim to see a wide range of teachers as soon as possible. This will help you to establish a sense of what is possible, what works, what doesn't work, what you would like to try yourself and what you would, perhaps, like to avoid.

The process lets you add detail to the conceptual map you hold in your mind concerning the nature of classroom teaching. As time progresses, this map will develop considerably, not least as a result of the teaching you do and the responses this engenders in students.

However, at the start of your training, the map will, inevitably, be sparsely populated. Giving yourself a wide range of observation experiences at the start of your training is therefore a good way to speed up your progress.

It is always worth seeing teachers who are known in the school as being particularly effective. It is also worth observing teachers who have particular strengths – behaviour management or questioning for example. Another useful approach is to see two or three teachers who employ contrasting approaches to achieve similar ends. Taking behaviour management as an example, you might see one teacher who creates a positive environment through remaining strict, another who works hard to build and maintain rapport, and a third who takes on more of an explicitly caring or nurturing role.

In this case, we have three approaches that are all equally valid. It will then be for you to decide whether you want to follow one in full, or take aspects from each.

You may also want to compare the approaches of newer and more experienced teachers. Both will offer ideas from which you can learn.

Crucially, as you observe more teaching and then combine this with your own experience of teaching, you will be increasingly able to discriminate between what is effective and what isn't, what is good and what is outstanding, and what suits you and what doesn't.

Turning back to wider notions of learning for a moment, this point offers a contextualisation of the ideas we looked at concerning knowledge and understanding. By conducting lots of observations and pooling the acquired knowledge with that which you derive from teaching your own lessons, you will be able to create an ever stronger base from which to develop your understanding.

Constructing such a base early on will make it easier for you to trial new ideas, develop a sense of what your teaching style is and, of course, plan and teach outstanding lessons.

Soft Skills

Our final category here is soft skills. These are the skills which employers of all types look for in prospective staff. They are also the things business leaders are forever deriding universities for failing to teach!

The term includes things such as teamwork, communication, independence, problem-solving, showing initiative, time management and decision making.

Considered another way, soft skills are tied up with an individual's emotional intelligence – their ability to read and understand situations, manage themselves and manage the interactions they have with other people.

When it comes to soft skills, it is worth remembering that a school is a place of work just like any other. The soft skills which are required to be successful – to be outstanding – are broadly similar to other workplaces, even if their application may differ given the unique context in which we find ourselves.

So, what do you need to do when it comes to soft skills?

The first thing is to be aware of them. Think about how you present yourself to the people in your training school – in terms of dress, manner and demeanour. Consider whether you are sufficiently proactive, whether you expect others to do things for you or whether you get on and do them yourself.

Ask yourself what you do when problems arise, whether you look at these as an opportunity or a difficulty. Question the extent to which you pay attention to the verbal and non-verbal signals given out by colleagues, as well as the signals you convey to others.

The next thing is to consider the image you want to present to those with whom you work. Take time to think about this before entering your first training school. And remember, this is a chance to present yourself however you wish. They do not know you, or what your professional manner is like. So decide what you want people to see and what you want people to think of you and then work hard to act accordingly.

Further down the line, when you are applying for jobs, being able to give concrete examples of your soft skills in action will put you in a strong position. Employers always prefer claims supported by evidence to those supported by waffle or those simply asserted but for which there appears to be no support.

With that in mind, here is a list of examples of things you can do during your training to demonstrate competence in various soft skills:

Teamwork: Plan lessons or a scheme of work with a colleague; team teach a series of lessons; offer your time to support members of your department or year group team; create and share resources with others.

Communication: Offer to deliver an assembly on an inspiring topic; create YouTube videos for your students communicating key pieces of content; attend parents' evenings and take part in report writing; plan a whole-school event (or get involved in the planning of one).

Problem-Solving: Reflect on why lessons don't go according to plan and then implement changes; create resources which solve a particular problem either for you or for your students; call on members of the pastoral team to help you deal with a behavioural issue; find innovative ways to personalise learning for individual students.

Independence: Plan a visit to another school to observe and talk to teachers working there; get involved in an extra-curricular activity; put on a workshop or series of workshops for students; write an article or blog post for an education media outlet.

Showing Initiative: Critically reflect on your own lessons – don't just wait to be told how to improve; call on the expertise of others to help you improve; ask senior colleagues to observe you and give feedback; attend education conferences or events; take part in online learning (www.tes.co.uk/courses).

Time Management: Plan your year in advance (see earlier); demonstrate you have managed your time effectively by using the excess you create to do other things (such as create excellent resources, develop your subject knowledge or take part in extra-curricular activities); develop systems for marking and planning which allow you to do both of these activities more quickly.

Decision-Making: Take on responsibility for planning a unit of work and then offer examples of how you chose what lessons to create, how to order the topic and how to effectively assess student learning; critically reflect on decisions you make in class and use this to inform future decision-making (you can then use these experiences to illustrate relevant points you make in an application).

Here we reach the conclusion to our practical overview. The aim has been to introduce some of the key things you will need to do and think about as you start to become a teacher, and to indicate how you can approach this in a way which helps you to become an outstanding trainee. We round matters off with some reflective questions and activities.

Questions

- What assumptions do you have about students, teaching and learning? What will you do if these assumptions prove to be false?

- Can you create a brief summary of what a trainee on your course needs to do to be graded outstanding? If not, what do you need to do or find out to be able to do this?

- If you were planning a curriculum for the age group you are training to teach, what would be on it and why?

- Does a curriculum need an aim or a series of aims to underpin its content? Why? And, if so, what should they be?

- What were you like as a student and what were your classmates like? What do you think caused you and your classmates to be like this?

Activities

- Audit your subject knowledge and compare this to the curriculum you will be teaching. Identify areas of strength, areas of weakness and any complete blanks. Think about what you can do to improve your knowledge.

- Observe a series of students in different lessons. Pay attention to their behaviour, their body language, how they interact with others, how they interact with the teacher and, of course, the learning they do. Consider how student behaviour differs – both between students and between lessons.

- Ask three or four senior colleagues in your training school to give you their golden rules for teaching success. Then, ask them why these are so important. Try to get underneath their suggestions, so as to get a sense of what their experience has taught them.

Chapter Four – Understanding Learners

Learners are our target audience. They are who we are trying to help. They are the reason teachers exist; the subjects at which teaching aims. Not all learners are the same, far from it. Although, many learners do have certain characteristics in common. As you become more experienced, you will begin to see students who feel familiar, even though you have not taught them before. This is usually an indication that their behaviour – how they act and think in your lessons – echoes that of a student you previously taught.

One of the most important things you must remember when working with students is that, if they exhibit behaviour which is not up to the standard you expect, it is the behaviour which needs to be addressed and highlighted as unacceptable, never the student.

This can be summed up in the mantra: focus on the behaviour, not the student.

Working in this way means you don't fall into the trap of labelling students (on which, more later) or giving students a sense that you see them as fundamentally bad or wrong. This message can easily be conveyed by accident if you are not careful; and it can sometimes unintentionally infect your thinking outside lessons.

For example, a student may stand up and shout out in one of your lessons before being disrespectful when you ask them to stop. Saying something like: 'You're bad for doing that' or 'Silly girls do things like that' immediately personalises the situation and suggests there is an inherent link between who the student is and the behaviour they are exhibiting.

It is much harder to change if we believe what we do is bound up with who we are.

So, instead, we can take the approach of saying: 'That behaviour isn't acceptable' or 'Stop doing that, you're capable of much better behaviour. I should know as I've seen it from you.' In these examples, we note that the behaviour is the focus, giving the student an opportunity to conceive of themselves behaving differently.

This is not to say we don't assign blame. In fact, the opposite. If we state that the behaviour is the issue, we also indicate that this behaviour is the result of a choice; a choice made by the student. On the other hand, if we unwittingly take the line of describing the student as the problem, we are in fact implying that they cannot be blamed. This is because it is illogical to blame a person for something they cannot help.

I mention this here, at the start of the chapter, because it is a way of thinking which neatly illustrates the principles underlying the points we will make in the following pages. These principles are:

- All learners are individuals

- All learners have the inherent capacity to learn, grow, change and develop

- All learners need to be helped to understand the norms expected in wider society

- All learners benefit from having teachers who consistently communicate high expectations

- All learners can make mistakes and this is one of the most important ways in which we learn

Classroom Management

For many trainee teachers, classroom management is a big concern. This is understandable. The link between good teaching and learning and good classroom management is self-evident. Learners need a stable, positive environment if they are to make progress. Behaviour which prevents this from being the case is problematic. It stifles progress.

It follows that, if you want to be an outstanding trainee teacher, you need to be able to cultivate an excellent atmosphere in your classroom. To put it another way, you need to become skilled in classroom management.

Anybody can do this. The giddy heights of effective behaviour management are accessible to all. It is not an exclusive club reserved for charismatic pedagogues or uber-stern taskmasters.

We will look at the whole topic of behaviour management in more detail in Chapter Ten. Here, I want to draw your attention to how understanding learners can help you to cultivate a positive, purposeful atmosphere.

The first thing to think about is the interactions you have with learners. Ask yourself what they will be seeing and hearing when you enter the classroom and then through the course of the lesson. Will they be seeing someone who is organised, prepared and in control? Will they hear someone who is happy to state what they expect and not to falter until it is achieved?

Students respond to positive messages of all types, including the positive message that you are ready to teach a well-planned lesson and to do so in a way which works for the benefit of everybody. On the other hand, many students will react differently if they see you are unprepared, disorganised or uncertain of what you are doing and why you are doing it.

This doesn't mean the only way to master classroom management is to get everything right. Far from it. But it does mean you can help yourself enormously by preparing carefully and developing a professional demeanour.

Simple things to do include photocopying resources the night before, arriving at the lesson early (wherever circumstances permit), having a starter activity ready to go straightaway and learning students' names as quickly as possible.

The second thing to think about is what will predispose students towards viewing you and your lessons positively. This includes everything mentioned previously, as well as communicating and maintaining clear boundaries, being polite, being positive and upbeat, showing interest in what students know and think, planning interesting activities and questions, giving students a degree of choice and control over their learning, and not talking down to or patronising them.

All of this is indicative of what makes people feel good generally. There isn't any great secret. It's in large part about fostering good relationships by attending to the needs and expectations students possess.

A case in point is the imposition and maintenance of clear boundaries. Many students when first asked will tell you they want to have fun in lessons and to be free to do what they want. However, nearly all these students, when pushed, will acknowledge that, realistically, this is not what they want, day after day, week after week. In fact, most students want to learn and to be successful. And most will openly admit that this motive of theirs is best met by a teacher who creates a focussed, purposeful atmosphere in which learning is central.

To further reinforce the point, try observing the same student in two lessons – one where classroom management is excellent and one where it needs improvement. You will probably see what almost amounts to two different students. And the one in the first classroom will feel they have achieved more and had a better experience than the one in the second.

Motives and Motivation

Appreciating that all learners have motives and varying degrees of motivation is key if you want to help them make as much progress as possible.

Human beings are subjects rather than objects. We have thoughts and feelings which cause us to do things. This is in contrast to objects, such as rocks, which have no consciousness through which to act.

Many motives exist. Some are familiar – love, greed, a desire for status, – and some are encountered more often through literature and film – obsession, megalomania, saving the universe.

We all have motives. Some of these are readily apparent; others may be hidden beneath the surface. Often, we do not pay attention to the motives driving our actions. Sometimes we identify them, marshal them and use our powers to achieve what it is we desire.

Motivation is heavily influenced by motive. If a strong motive exist within us, it is likely that this will drive our motivation to do certain things. Witness, for example, the student whose motive is to become a doctor. The motivation they show in lessons and when working at home is a testament to what they are aiming to fulfil. Similarly, consider the young child who continually pulls herself up using the settee until, eventually, she can stand unaided. The motive here – to be able to stand up – motivates the behaviour.

All learners are subjects. All learners have motives and these motives inform their levels of motivation.

As a trainee teacher, thinking about this fact will help you to empathise with the position in which students find themselves. This, in turn, will give you a better insight into how you can motivate them and what you can do in your lessons to help them achieve their goals.

The flipside of this is that you may identify a lack of motivation or an absence of desirable motives connected to learning. If you make such discoveries (and undoubtedly you will from time to time) you are in a position to do something about this. It could involve finding novel ways to motivate students or talking to them about motives they might have and linking these to the learning they do in school. In the latter case, the aim is to help students see how working hard and doing their best can help them to achieve their goals, even if they do not yet realise this fact.

Being aware of motive also helps you to think yourself into students' thought processes. From here, you can begin to unpick the behaviour you witness and start to think about the best way to alter or reinforce it.

For example, let us imagine we have a young child who frequently calls out in class. After the lesson, we sit down and start to think about the motives underpinning this behaviour. What does calling out achieve, we wonder. How does it alter the classroom situation from what would otherwise be the case?

This might lead us to the theory that calling out draws attention and affords a certain kind of status. We might then conclude that moving the child in question to the front of the class and making a point of working with them at the beginning of tasks will help to fulfil these motives but in a far more positive sense than what we are presently seeing.

Another point to consider when it comes to motivation is the difference between intrinsic and extrinsic motivation. The latter is inspired by things external to us while the former is linked to things which are internal.

Extrinsic motivation includes being motivated to win a prize or to collect an award. Such aims are often worthy. However, motivation tends to drop significantly as soon as the goal has been achieved. Worse, motivation to achieve the same goal in the future, again and again, tends to be low. For this reason, extrinsic motivation is often not sustained over time.

Intrinsic motivation is somewhat different. It involves the fulfilment of goals which are internal to us – which form a part of who we are. For example, a learner may have a desire to work hard because they believe that working hard is important. Thus, their actions are an attempt to both reinforce their conception of what matters and to meet that belief by marrying their actions to it.

For these reasons, intrinsic motivation tends to be more powerful and more sustainable. Although it is also harder to cultivate.

To be outstanding trainee teacher I would suggest experimenting with extrinsic and intrinsic motivation so you can see the effects for yourself. Having done this, look to develop a sense of intrinsic motivation in the classes you teach.

The easiest way to do this is to build rapport with students, communicate high expectations and continually reinforce the message that everybody can learn and make progress by applying themselves and taking on board feedback. Acting in this way will serve to establish a culture in which your students internalise these messages – helping them to become intrinsically motivated as they then seek to meet the positive expectations they have about themselves and their capacity to learn.

Naturally this takes time, but the results, as noted, will be significant; particularly when contrasted to the temporary effects achieved by offering prizes or rewards.

Seeing Individuals

This is harder than it sounds, especially when you first start working with a class or a number of different classes.

Having thirty faces in front of you can be daunting. Even if it is not, you will still find yourself in a position where there is more information coming at you than you can reasonably take in (names, faces, behaviour, evidence of prior learning and so on).

Given such a situation, the ordinary reaction is often to view your class as a mass, or as a series of groups (quiet ones, loud ones, more-able ones). This is the application of a process with which we are all familiar: finding ways to make sense of more information than we can easily process in one go.

You will note that the division of the class into groups is, in essence, a rough attempt at classification, which echoes one of the central aspects of human thought more generally. When we encounter that which is new, we try to understand it in part by seeing if it will fit into the existing categories we possess. As an aside, philosophers have argued that concepts *and* categories form the basis of our thought, with both being necessary constituents of the foundations upon which our thinking rests.

But I digress.

For our purposes – becoming an outstanding trainee teacher – it is important we are alive to the likelihood that we will not see all students as individuals at first. And that we need to work hard to correct this state of affairs.

Doing so will bring many benefits.

The relationships you cultivate with your students will be better if you see each learner as an individual. You will be able to personalise how you talk to them and reflect back the sense that you know who they are, what they are like and that they are important.

Seeing learners as individuals means building a picture of what they are like, both in general and in the specific context of learning. This information allows you to tailor your teaching to better meet their needs.

For example, if you know that a particular student struggles to get started when faced with a piece of writing, you can act on this. Even better, if you come to understand that the student struggles for reasons quite specific to them, you can tailor your support even more precisely.

Returning to the theme of motive and motivation, seeing learners as individuals helps you to gain a better understanding of these two facets of their characters. Armed with accurate, specific information about individual motives and motivation places you in a far stronger position than if you possess only vague, undifferentiated information which you apply to the class as a whole.

We all like to feel important. This does not mean we all need to be held up as the centre of attention. Feeling important stems in large part from feeling noticed. Feeling noticed means we feel that others see us as who we are – an individual. Learning names, working to understand prior knowledge, paying attention to students' characters: all of this helps you to learn about students as individuals. From here, you can show them that you think they are important. This is highly motivational.

A brief word of warning before we move on. While you are training, you will spend less time with students than when you come to work as a teacher proper. This means you may not have as much opportunity as you would like to get to know students as individuals.

There are three useful methods you can employ to overcome this difficulty.

First, get hold of information regarding the classes you will be teaching from other sources. This includes the people who teach them already, their form tutors if appropriate, the recording and reporting system used in school (often SIMS), the special educational needs (SEN) register (maintained by the special educational needs coordinator, or SENCO) and any other internal recording systems.

Second, when observing the teacher or teachers whose lessons you will take over, use this as an opportunity to observe and interact with the students as well. Start gathering information from the moment you step into the room. Look at behaviour, look at learning and listen for names. During activities, circulate through the room and help different groups.

Ask the teacher if there are specific students with whom they would like you to work. Observe how the teacher interacts with their class and see what kind of support they give to different learners.

Third, take a look at the work students are producing. How much there is and how accessible it is will vary depending on the time of year and the subject or age groups with whom you are working. Suffice to say, however, you will always be able to get your hands on something students have produced. Examine this. See if it tallies with the perceptions you are starting to build. In the case of written work, ask yourself whether it matches the oral contributions of the student. Compare work produced by different students and use this as a means to analyse where you think individual learners are at in relation to their peers.

These endeavours – gathering information about learners, their needs, abilities and characters – is important when first meeting a class. It allows you to see them as individuals more quickly than would otherwise be the case.

It also echoes one of the jobs outstanding teachers do every time they teach and mark: collect information on their students' learning. This information can then be used to tailor teaching so it has an ever higher degree of relevance and personalisation.

The Relationship between Teachers and Learners

When starting out as a teacher, it is important to remember that you are the professional in the room. Your relationship with students should be friendly, but in no way should you seek to be their friend. This sums up nicely the importance of creating a positive atmosphere while also maintaining professional distance.

Boundaries are a vital part of the relationships you cultivate. These boundaries should be set by you and not the other way round. Whatever boundaries you set out, expect learners to test them. This is what children do! It is a part of the wider learning they engage in at school. Consider in advance how you will respond when students push boundaries. For example, if you ask for silence during a task and students begin to talk, what will you do? Rehearsing responses to situations such as these is great because it gives you the confidence to be firm and assertive where necessary. It also helps you to avoid becoming flustered and diminishes the likelihood of an emotional response emerging within the heat of the lesson.

Relationships develop over time. Therefore, you should expect teaching to become easier as you get to know your students better. We noted above some of the things you can do to speed up this process.

To be an outstanding trainee, you will want to develop outstanding relationships. Such relationships usually rest on a few key things.

Enthusiasm is the first of these. It is infectious. If you display it, your students will pick up on this and respond positively. Enthusiasm can be seen in your body language and heard in your voice. It can also be communicated through the type of lessons you create.

Manners, politeness and good humour are next. These are ways of acting which support the success of any social enterprise. And, as we mentioned in Chapter One, teaching is very much a social enterprise, being predicated in large part on the interactions which take place in the classroom.

Organisation and a sense of purpose come third. Students arrive at lessons expecting to have an experience to which they are accustomed. That is, in most schools, a lesson with a clear objective, connecting to what they have done previously and introducing ideas or information which are new. You are unlikely to be cut much slack because you are training. To most students, such a concept is hard to properly grasp (they might know what the word means, but understanding is likely to be limited due to their lack of wider experience).

A sense of purpose gives lessons drive and meaning. This is engaging for students. It makes them feel like what they are doing is worthwhile in itself – and is not just designed to serve an instrumental end.

Finally, most good relationships are characterised by consistency (albeit sometimes broken up by spontaneity). Consistency helps us to know where we are with somebody. It lets us predict the future with a reasonable degree of accuracy and, in the case of learners, allows them to be successful in the eyes of the teacher. This is because they come to know your expectations, boundaries and ways of working, meaning they can adapt their behaviour to fit with these.

An inconsistent teacher creates problems for students, leading to deteriorating relationships and a sense of frustration on both sides. This frustration stems from the fact that neither teacher nor learners feel like their expectations are being met.

Simple rapport building techniques through which you can hasten the development of positive relationships include:

- Learning names quickly. If this is difficult for you, ask students to make name cards they display at the front of their desks.

- Talking in terms of us instead of you and them. For example: This lesson we're going to be looking at what happened in Pompeii. As opposed to: This lesson you will be looking at what happened in Pompeii.

- Giving genuine, specific praise, highlighting things students have done well.

- Thanking students for answers, contributions and working hard. This includes thanking the class as a whole at the end of a lesson.

- Greeting students at the start of the lesson. If possible, ensure books are on desks, a starter activity is on the board and then stand at the door to welcome learners into the classroom.

- Making your expectations clear from the beginning, communicating these regularly and sticking to them.

- Creating lessons which give students the opportunity to be successful. This includes sharing success criteria and showing what success looks like.

- Asking students questions and listening to what they say.

- When behaviour is poor, focussing on the behaviour rather than the student.

- Planning interesting lessons in which learners have a leading role.

- Planning lessons which stretch and challenge all learners.

- Remaining positive and enthusiastic (even if you don't feel like it!).

Expectations

The expectations you communicate to learners have a profound effect on how they see you, themselves and their learning. High expectations ought to be maintained at all times – both in regard to what you think learners capable of achieving and how you expect them to interact with you and with each other.

Outstanding trainee teachers bring a sense of urgency into the classroom with them. This breaks down into a clear indication – through the lessons they create and the manner in which they conduct themselves – that challenge is for everybody and that everybody, through the application of effort and persistence, is capable of achieving well.

To illustrate how vital high expectations are, consider what a classroom is like in which expectations are low.

In such a place, the teacher is easily satisfied, the students do not have much to live up to and the whole enterprise of learning is conducted without pace or any sense of purpose.

Being in such a classroom on a regular basis is soporific at best, highly dispiriting at worst.

You should think about the expectations you have for your learners prior to starting to teach them. This way, you can refine and clarify what you want, before communicating this from the off.

A good tip is to think about processes, rather than products. Starting from the premise that you expect all learners to achieve an 'A' is generally foolish. In the vast majority of cases this, or something similar, will not be feasible; your intentions, while good, may even be counterproductive.

If we look at processes instead, we find ourselves in a more tenable position. Our premise might be that we expect all learners to work hard from the beginning of the lesson through to the end. It does not matter what prior achievement students possess – this is an expectation they will all be able to meet. The process, in this case, is the application of effort.

Another example is an expectation that no student gives up when they encounter a problem. First they should try to solve it, perhaps by implementing two or three strategies they have previously learned. Again, this is about a process rather than a product. Our expectation is not that all students will solve all problems they encounter. Rather, it is that they will endeavour to try, by applying their knowledge and understanding to whatever is at issue.

You can communicate your expectations to students in a number of ways.

First, you can do so explicitly by telling them what you want, why it matters and how they can achieve it. Second, you can do so by praising behaviour and thinking which meets or exceeds your expectations. This reinforces the behaviour or thinking in question and, if done publically, serves as a model for other students to copy. Third, you can do so implicitly through your body language, the lessons you plan, the questions you ask and the type of learning you facilitate within your classroom.

In addition, you should be aware that, at times, you may need to challenge the expectations learners bring to your lessons, regarding themselves, their learning and their relationship to you. For example, a learner may consistently denigrate their own abilities through the language they use to talk about themselves and their work. Picking up on this, rephrasing the learner's speech and giving them a new vocabulary with which to speak will help to alter the way in which they think.

In summary, then, your expectations are conveyed through everything you do in the classroom, as well as through the lessons you plan and, to a slightly lesser extent, the marking you do. Attending to them and being alive to the importance of continually reinforcing them will help you to be outstanding. In the process, it will help you to lift your students up, taking them further than might otherwise be the case and giving them the tools to make great progress and to believe in themselves and their own potential.

Labelling and Blank Slates

Our final thoughts prior to concluding deal with a point somewhat smaller than those previously enumerated but nonetheless important.

Labelling is the process through which we attach labels to individuals or groups. We see it in the media on a regular basis and most of us do it to some degree in our daily lives. Walking through town we might see a group of young men wearing hoodies and, almost involuntarily, find ourselves labelling them as potentially menacing. The newspapers may repeatedly preface a politician's name with an adjective, in the process labelling them and characterising them according to that one epithet in the process. Red Ed (Ed Miliband) is one example.

The danger of labelling is that it attaches a certain status (usually negative) to the group or individual in question. This, in turn, leads us to see them primarily through that label. Thus, we fail to see them as individuals or groups of individuals. And, more importantly, we start treating them in accordance with the connotations of the label, rather than in accordance with the reality of our interactions with them.

From this, imagine a student who a teacher labels as a bad influence. This labelling may stem from true experiences. But those experiences would have been of the student's behaviour, not of the student's essential self. In this case, the labelling of the student makes it much harder for them to alter their behaviour. The teacher who attributes the label has, in so doing, written off the possibility of change. What is more, that teacher will then view the student in question through the prism of the label, reinforcing the power of the attribution and encouraging the student to live up to it.

For these reasons, it is important to avoid labelling students wherever possible. Instead, focus on the behaviour and what the student needs to do, if necessary, to alter that behaviour.

A corollary of this approach is that you should try to treat every lesson as a blank slate. When learners arrive, give them the opportunity to start again. Avoid labelling them with their prior behaviour as soon as they enter the classroom.

Two caveats attach themselves to this point. First, a blank slate is not possible if prior behaviour was unacceptable and has not yet been dealt with. In this situation, the primary aim is to deal with the behaviour first so as to demonstrate that actions have consequences.

Second, I am not arguing here that you should forget what has happened in previous lessons. Rather, that unless you give learners a chance to behave better than they did previously, making any kind of change will be hard for them to achieve.

And that draws this chapter to a close. All that remains is to point you in the direction of the questions and activities beneath, each of which will help you to think further about how you can best understand your learners.

Questions

- What does it feel like to be a learner? What memories do you have from your own experience of being a learner? How might your experiences differ from those of other people?

- Do we have a moral duty to see each other as individuals? Why?

- To what extent do the expectations you have about yourself limit what you are capable of achieving? Do you accept that expectations play such a significant part in learning? Why?

- What motives underpin your behaviour? Do you accept that motivation is directly connected to the motives or desires people possess? Can a motive or a desire be possessed? Or would another word be more appropriate?

- What were your relationships with teachers like at school? How did these affect you?

Activities

- When observing colleagues in your training school, examine how they build and sustain rapport with students. Make a note of the different techniques you see teachers employing and reflect on whether you would feel comfortable using these yourself.

- Walk around your training school. Focus on observing what expectations are conveyed to students. Look at displays, look into classrooms, survey the building itself. Having done this, consider what impact spending 30+ hours a week in such an environment might have.

- Read through a daily newspaper and see what labels you can spot. Look for labels attached to individuals and groups. Ask yourself how these labels shape your perception of the people being written about. From here, go on to think about how the process of labelling could affect learners with whom you are familiar – either from having taught them or from having observed them in a lesson.

Chapter Five – Unpicking the Lesson

In this chapter we turn to the unit through which teachers work: the lesson. It is in the lesson that teaching and learning primarily takes place. It follows that the structure of the lesson – how it is planned and how it is designed – influences what the teacher does and what students are asked or able to do.

Lessons come in a range of shapes and sizes. But, in general, they are largely similar. There is a purpose, designated by the teacher, which informs the structure. This structure can be broken down into sections and those sections help students to learn; ideally this involves an increasing degree of challenge, pushing students to work harder and to think more deeply so they maximise their progress.

Here, we will look at all the important constituents of the lesson, providing analysis as well as practical examples for you to try out.

Structure

Think of lessons as like a story. They have a beginning, a middle and an end. These three elements go together to form the structure of the lesson; the story the teacher is seeking to tell.

It is helpful to conceive of lessons in this way for two reasons. First it allows us to keep in mind the fact that we are always working towards something. This is usually the increased knowledge and/or understanding of our students, or an improved capacity to do a certain thing (the practice and development of skills).

Second, stories are like journeys. And learning is essentially a journey. When we learn, we move from a starting point of existing capacity and, when the learning is complete, we find ourselves in an end position from which it is clear that our capacities have improved.

Thus, when planning your lessons, you ought always to keep in mind a sense of where you are going. Remind yourself that you have an end in mind – something you want your students to be able to do or know. Having this as your guiding light ensures the structure of your lesson helps students to achieve the end you have specified. Failing to take account of the end means risking aspects of your lesson drifting away from what you are trying to achieve.

To put it another way, the structure of your lesson should be subordinate to what you are trying to achieve. When planning a lesson, always remember that the plan is nothing more than your way of ensuring students achieve what you want them to achieve.

From here we can see that lesson structure is not an end in itself but a means. It is framework through which learning can happen, not learning itself. This is an obvious point. However, one of the most common pitfalls new teachers encounter is the desire for perfection. When planning a lesson they want to create something that is perfect and without fault. This is impossible. No lesson is perfect and no lesson can be planned to ensure all faults are avoided.

Succumbing to the desire for perfectionism is understandable. It stems from laudable aims – the desire to create something which is good for students. But it is counterproductive and unrealistic. It privileges the structure of the lesson – all that which you focus on during your planning – over the learning students do.

This is because you cannot plan the learning students do in advance of the lesson. You can only plan what you will teach and how you anticipate this will stimulate and facilitate learning.

And in this point we find the crux. No lesson plan can be perfect because no lesson plan actually involves any student learning. It is only when we put our lesson into action that learning happens. Therefore, the perfect structure is a mirage, because how students interact with that structure is unknown prior to us turning it into a reality by teaching it.

When planning lessons, the best advice is to think at all times about your end point and to keep asking yourself whether the structure you are developing will give students the best chance of achieving this. If the answer is 'yes', you're onto a winner. If the answer is 'no', you can change things. Either way, student learning, rather than the search for a perfect lesson, will be the driving force in your thinking.

Purpose

Implicit in what we said above is the idea that great lessons have a clear purpose. That purpose, in a broad sense, ought always to be the maximisation of learning. In a specific sense, it will vary depending on what is being taught and to whom.

So, for example, if we are planning a lesson for a Year 7 Religious Studies class, our general purpose will be to create something which maximises their learning, while our specific purpose might be to increase their knowledge and understanding of Buddhism.

We can see then that all lessons aim at the same goal, but that the goal does not always appear in the same clothing. An A Level PE teacher and a Year 3 teacher both have the same goal of maximising learning when they sit down and plan their respective lessons, but that goal is dressed up differently for each of them, the clothes being those appropriate for the age group and the curriculum.

If you try to plan a lesson without a clear purpose in mind you will run into difficulties. The first problem you will face will be a lack of direction. The second will be a lack of criteria through which to judge the efficacy of the structure you are building.

Let us look at an example to demonstrate this.

A Year 6 teacher sits down to plan a literacy lesson. They know they want to plan something around sentence structure but have no clearer purpose than that. Immediately they find their mind pulling in all sorts of different directions. The creative aspect of this is neutered by the fact that no direction can be easily preferred because the purpose remains undefined. Every judgement the teacher tries to make concerning whether an idea would be useful or not is undermined by the fact they do not have any criteria with which to make the judgement. Rather, the criteria are unspecified or too vague to be useful.

Compare this to another teacher who decides the purpose of their lesson is to give students practice in applying grammar rules to a series of different paragraphs and sentences before going on to create their own grammar challenges with which to test their peers.

Clearly this second teacher would be able to marshal their lesson structure to fulfil their purpose. Every decision they make during the planning process can be vetted against the criteria of to what extent it will help students achieve the learning the teacher has specified.

This comparison illustrates the significant benefits which accrue when we define and clarify the purpose of our lesson before we start to plan. In effect, we are working through the myriad options open to us, settling on one, and then using this to inform everything else we do.

It leads to our structure being determined by our desire to reach the end we have specified. Namely, fulfilment of our purpose.

In short, turning the general goal of maximising learning into a highly specific goal, relevant for our students and the curriculum, gives us a clear purpose. This purpose then informs all decisions we make as part of our planning, allowing us to tailor the structure of our lesson in a way that helps us to achieve our purpose.

The golden rule of lesson planning is thus to begin by identifying and clarifying your purpose.

Aims, Objectives and Outcomes

The purpose on which you settle is for you and your students. It is the driving force of your planning; the lens through which you look at what you are doing.

Beyond this, you will be asked to specify other guiding principles, some of which you will share with students and some of which you will not.

The three most common words you will come across in this area are aims, objectives and outcomes. As a trainee teacher, the difference between these can be difficult to grasp. That is because the differences are not great. Think of them as differences of degree, rather than of type.

To assist you in your planning, let me provide a set of clear definitions from which you can work:

Lesson Purpose: As noted above, this is what you are trying to achieve. It is the end point of your lesson; where you are trying to take your students.

Lesson Aims: Aims are the specific things which make up your purpose. So, for example, you might break your purpose down into three aims. If these aims are fulfilled, the purpose has been achieved.

Lesson Objective: This is what you want students to be able to do by the end of the lesson. It is the objective you and they share. It will usually be the end point you identified as your purpose, rewritten into language students can easily grasp.

Lesson/Learning Outcomes: These are the things students will be able to do by the end of the lesson. If they can do them, they will have achieved the objective, met the aims and achieved the purpose of the lesson. The extent to which any one student fulfils the outcomes will vary (one may fulfil to a high standard, another to a lower standard).

As clear as mud, then!

I joke; you can see, hopefully, from the above definitions, that there is a qualitative difference between each term. The proliferation of terms is as much down to administrative developments as anything else. Each one has its own history when it comes to lesson planning – a history it is not useful to go into here.

Suffice to say, when planning a lesson:

- Identify your purpose

- Break this down into a series of aims

- Create a plan

- Write a lesson objective which students can understand

- And, finally, consider what outcomes you expect to see if students have been hugely successful, mildly successful and reasonably successful.

You will note that I advocate writing the objective and outcomes after planning the lesson. This is because you will have your purpose to guide you and it is this purpose which, as we noted above, is closely bound up with the learning you are seeking to achieve. Trying to design a lesson which fits in with a purpose, a set of aims, an objective and a set of outcomes is nigh on impossible. The amount of things you need to satisfy is too great. It stymies creativity.

Instead, work on the basis that your purpose is enough. When the lesson is planned, look at what objective and outcomes it gives rise to, safe in the knowledge that these will be sufficient, because all your planning has been driven by the purpose you first specified.

Content

We move now to think about the content of our lessons, before going on to examine the elements which commonly constitute the structure of any plan: starters, activities and plenaries.

As we have said, the content of our lessons will be largely determined by the curriculum we have been asked to teach, as well as our students' prior learning.

For an individual lesson, our thinking will need to encompass a number of questions. These are as follows:

- What have my students already studied?

- What else do they need to study as part of this unit of work?

- How does this link to the wider curriculum?

- What do they already know about the topic?

- In an ideal world, what would I like them to know, understand and be able to do?

These questions will help you to clarify what content should be included in the lesson you are planning. You can come back to them time and again as a useful planning tool. Over time, you will come to internalise them and be able to recall them at will.

As a trainee, it is likely you will be asked to teach lessons which form part of an existing scheme of work.

A scheme of work is just as it sounds – a sequence of lessons planned by a teacher to cover an extended period of time. This could be a fortnight, a term or longer.

To start creating outstanding lessons, the first thing we need to do is get hold of any existing schemes of work which are relevant to the classes we will be teaching. From here we can quickly see what students have already done (and, therefore, what we can expect them to know and understand) as well as where the teacher envisages them going next.

Our second task is to compare the scheme(s) of work to the wider curriculum. You will remember that this is provided by the government, by an exam board or by the school. In making this comparison our aim is to get a sense of how the current lessons – including the ones we will be planning and teaching – fit into the wider scheme of things.

Gaining this knowledge makes it easier for us to understand what content is relevant for the lesson(s) we are planning as well as whether or not we can make links and connections to what students already know and to what they will be studying in the future.

When it comes to the content of lessons, greater expertise concerning what needs to be taught, why it needs to be taught and how it relates to other areas of the curriculum will always allow you to make better decisions than if you do not have this information.

A few further points to think about before we move on.

First, if you have clearly defined the purpose of your lesson, you will be in a good position to appreciate what the content needs to be. This is because students will have to learn about specific things if they are to successfully achieve your purpose.

Second, it will take time for you to gain an accurate understanding of how much content fits into a single lesson. I know this might not be what you want to hear! However, there are no hard and fast rules about how much is the right amount.

Your understanding will develop as you plan and teach lessons. Each time you do this you will be able to assess whether there is too much content for students to deal with, too little, or the right amount. You can speed the process up by actively attending to what happens in your lessons, by observing the impact the level of content has on your students and by spending a little time afterwards critically reflecting (for more on which, see below).

Third, and finally, it is always worth starting simply before increasing the level of complexity. So, for example, you might begin by introducing students to one idea or important piece of information. When they have grasped this, increase the level of challenge by bringing in a wider range of information and ideas, or things which are more complex and require deeper explanation.

Learning rests on prior knowledge. Giving students a simple entry-point means that, when they encounter content which is deeper, broader, more specific or more complex, they can meet this from a position of strength.

Lesson Framework

So, we have our purpose, we are using this to inform our decision-making, we've selected the content we want to cover and, from this, we are developing a clear sense of what the lesson is going to involve; what story we are going to tell.

In other words, the learning we are seeking to create is starting to take shape.

Our next task is to work out how we will ask students to engage with the content in order to achieve our purpose.

This is where we plan the separate elements of the lesson. The things we and the students will actually do in the classroom.

As you may already be aware, there is a standard and widely-used lesson framework. It is likely that you will be expected to learn and apply this model. It goes as follows:

- Starter

- Main Activities

- Plenary

Here, I will briefly explain how this model works, as well as what constitutes each element. Below, I will give practical examples of each for you to try out in your teaching.

The premise for the framework is simple. It runs something like this:

Students come into the room and are introduced to the lesson topic through an accessible yet challenging starter activity. This gives students a chance to be successful, pushes their thinking and gets them focussed on learning. One or more main activities follow. These give students the chance to interact with the content. It is here that the majority of the teaching and learning takes place. Finally, the plenary is an opportunity to reinforce the learning which has taken place. Within the plenary, the teacher helps students to reflect on, revisit and apply their learning.

Main activities are often thought of as episodes. These episodes are sequential and become increasingly challenging. This ensures students have their thinking stretched throughout the course of the lesson.

Other lesson frameworks exist and, while that outlined above is widely felt to be successful, this method is not the be all and end all. Nonetheless, it is a useful, uncomplicated approach – one that you will need to become familiar with as you strive to be outstanding.

My own advice is to concentrate on mastering the three-part lesson to begin with (for that, for good or for ill(!), is the name this framework has been given…for obvious reasons). As your training progresses and you feel increasingly confident in planning and teaching three-part lessons, play around with the framework and see what other ideas you can come up with.

Doing this will help you to keep challenging yourself. It will also cause you to think more critically about the nature of lesson planning and the skills you have developed.

Starters

We turn now to starter activities. These are the activities through which we begin a lesson. They should be accessible for all students but should also contain a good level of challenge. The aim is to facilitate success but also to push students to think further than they might be inclined to do on their own.

Facilitating success binds students into the lesson and fosters motivation. An immediate sense of challenge sets the tone for the lesson as a whole.

Here are five examples of starter activities:

List It: Give students the lesson topic and ask them to list as many things as possible connected to it. Provide a time limit to create a sense of pace. Challenge students by asking them to put the things on their list into a series of groups or to pick out and justify the three most important things they write down.

If this is the answer, what might be the question?: Present students with an answer connected to the lesson topic. Ask them to work on their own or with a partner to come up with two or three possible questions for which this could be the right answer. Challenge students by asking them to explain why they think you have chosen this specific answer or by asking them to rank their questions from best to worst (and to provide justification).

A-Z: Students work in pairs. They write the letters A-Z on a sheet of paper. You introduce the lesson topic. Students then have 3-5 minutes to identify a word connected to the topic for each letter of the alphabet. The first pair to complete their A-Z are the winners. Challenge students by giving a series of caveats such as: at least three words must be concepts, or, at least one letter must have a phrase rather than a word attached to it.

Paired Discussion: Display a question or series of questions on the board connected to the topic and invite students to discuss these with a partner. Set a time limit and ask one member of each group to make a note of the points discussed. Challenge students by asking them to discuss the questions from someone else's perspective or by asking them to develop their own questions.

Stimulus Image: Display a striking or unusual image on the board which connects to the topic. Ask students to look at the image in silence and to think about it. Ask them to note down their thoughts and then to share these with a partner. If appropriate, provide one or two questions which will help students think about the image. Challenge students by asking them to speculate as to why the image was taken, what might have happened before and what might have happened afterwards.

As you will note, each activity grabs students' attention, gives them an opportunity to be successful in relation to the learning and then challenges them to think further.

Try these starters out and see how you get on!

Activities

Main activities vary considerably. Think of them as vessels for content. You decide what content you want students to learn. Then you choose the activities into which this will fit best.

How you make this decision depends on the topic you are teaching, the age group you are working with and your own personal preferences.

Good activities give students plenty of opportunity to actively engage with content. They are challenging and also allow for active practice. Finally, they are differentiated. This means that students can access them and learn through them regardless of their ability levels and prior attainment. We will look at differentiation further in Chapter Seven. Here, we will simply say that it means doing things and planning things which allow all students to access the learning and make progress.

With these thoughts in mind, here are five examples of effective activities:

Jigsaw: Divide the class into groups of five. Each group is given a different part of the topic to research. The teacher provides suitable materials and a time limit is set. When the time is up each group is numbered off 1-5. That is, the first student is number one, the second number two and so on. New groups are formed. All the number ones get together, all the number twos get together and so on. In these new groups, students take it in turns to teach each other what they learned while in their original groups.

Speed Debating: The class is divided in half. A statement is displayed on the board. Half the class will argue for the statement while half will argue against. Each half is divided into smaller groups and students are given time to prepare their arguments. When the time is up, pairs are formed. Each pair contains one student who is for and one student who is against. Debates take place concurrently in a two minute time-slot. When the time is up, the students who are for stand up and find a new partner. The debate is repeated with the new pairings. The process is repeated as many times as the teacher feels is appropriate.

Stepped Practice: Present students with a series of tasks or questions which allow them to practice a skill or practice applying something they have learned. The tasks or questions should get progressively more difficult. This is where the 'stepped' element comes in. As students work through the activity, their thinking is increasingly challenged. Different students will get to different points; all will have their thinking stretched.

Options: Teach students about something connected to the topic and present a range of options through which they might respond to the material. For example, you might spend ten minutes explaining to students why Macbeth acted in the way he did before inviting students to respond to this by creating an alternative interpretation, an imaginary interview with Macbeth or a piece of first-person narration from the perspective of Macbeth or another key character. Here, the aim is to give students choice so that they can self-select and, through doing, engage with the content at an appropriate level.

Learn – Experiment – Reflect: Teach students about something connected to the topic and then provide them with the tools or guidance necessary to experiment with this knowledge. For example, you might teach students about the nature of friction before giving them a series of toy trucks and surface types which they can use to conduct relevant experiments. When sufficient time has passed, lead students in a reflection. This reflection should focus on the relationship between what students initially learned and what they discovered in their experiments.

Each of these activities can be adapted to work with a variety of different topics, subjects and age-groups. This illustrates the initial point that good activities are vessels into which different content can be placed.

Plenaries

Plenaries come at the end of the lesson. Ideally, they should be between five and fifteen minutes in length. This will generally be determined by the overall length of the lesson. A two hour lesson may warrant a fifteen minute plenary. A thirty-five minute lesson will not!

The aim here is to help students reinforce their learning by revisiting it in some manner. This can include reflecting on it, using it and questioning it.

Here are some example plenaries to illustrate the point:

- Identify three things you know or can do now that you didn't know or couldn't do at the start of the lesson.

- How would you explain your learning today to someone who knew nothing about the topic?

- Use your learning from today's lesson to answer these questions about the topic.

In each case, we are directing students to think about their learning and to use it in some way. The active engagement which this precipitates helps to reinforce the learning in students' minds. It also give you a chance to check the learning students have done and to intervene if any misconceptions have developed.

In addition, you can use the information you elicit through the plenary to inform your subsequent lesson planning. If, for example, the plenary reveals students are struggling to accurately apply a particular idea, then you can plan to revisit this at the start of the following lesson.

Plenaries tend to fall into two general categories. On the one hand, they ask students to reflect on their learning (as in examples one and two above). On the other hand, they ask students to use their learning (as in examples two and three – two, of course, straddles both categories).

The type of plenary you choose to use will depend on your students and what you want from the end of your lesson. The best advice is to play around with a range of examples and see what works for you.

So there we have it, a guide to lesson planning. We identify our purpose, use this as the basis of our decision-making, select our content and then choose a starter activity, one, two or three main activities and a plenary. Having done this, we clarify our objectives and outcomes and then…we're done!

Well, not quite.

Reflection

The final element of outstanding lesson planning comes after we have taught our lesson. It is reflection.

Critical reflection (as opposed to uncritical reflection in which all lessons are simply brilliant!) involves sitting down and thinking honestly about what happened in the lesson, how this relates to what we expected to happen, and what we think we can learn from the experience.

Generally, trainee teachers find it easier to focus on the problems they encountered while teaching a lesson. But remember, honest reflection means giving a realistic account of everything that happened – good, bad and indifferent.

Failing to do this will limit the efficacy of your reflection. This, in turn, will slow your progress and make it harder for you to become an outstanding trainee teacher.

A useful exercise is to take a set of questions and select three or four of these at random. The questions you choose then from the basis of your reflection. This way, you do not have to worry about your own objectivity – the process of random selection will do the work for you.

Here is a set of twelve numbered questions you can use as the basis of this exercise:

1. What went well in the lesson and why?

2. If you could alter one thing about the lesson, what would it be and why?

3. How much progress do you feel students made? How could they have made more?

4. What will you use again? Will you adapt or develop it at all?

5. Did the lesson develop as you expected? Why?

6. How successful do you feel your activities were? What learning did they give rise to?

7. How did different groups of students respond to the lesson? What can you learn from this?

8. Which part of the lesson went closest to plan and which was the furthest off? Why do you think this was the case?

9. What did you do during the lesson? What did the students do?

10. How did your activity choices influence the flow of the lesson and the classroom atmosphere?

11. What problems did you encounter and why do you think they arose?

12. What advice would you give yourself based on the lesson? Be specific and constructive.

Reflection needn't be a lengthy process. Regularity is more important than length. The key is to get into a routine of reviewing your lessons critically, on a regular basis. This ensures you keep making improvements, speeding up your development. The results will quickly become apparent. Even if they are only incremental at first, the important thing is that they will be there for you to see.

We finish the chapter with a set of questions, as well as three activities which will help you to think further about lessons and lesson planning.

Questions

- What lessons, if any, do you remember from school? Why do you remember them? And, if you don't remember any, is this necessarily a bad thing?

- To what extent should a teacher be prepared to change their lesson plan in response to their students? If they do decide to make changes, how can they be sure the intended learning still takes place?

- Earlier, I suggested the perfect lesson is an illusion. Do you agree? Is it ever possible to plan a perfect lesson?

- Why might it be useful to think through a lesson plan from the perspective of a student – or from the perspective of a series of different students?

- Can all learning be anticipated by the teacher, or does some happen by accident? What are the consequences of this for lesson planning?

Activities

- Observe two or three colleagues. Ask them to provide you with a lesson plan or, at the least, a rough sketch of what they plan to do with their class. Examine how the lesson they teach compares with their plan.

- Find another trainee who has some time available then sit down and plan a lesson together. Talk about the process as you go. Ask each other questions, including about why certain decision have been made. Don't be afraid to challenge each other or suggest alternatives. At the end of the exercise, reflect on what you have learned from each other.

- Set up a focus group of students and invite them to plan a lesson or a series of lessons with you. Give them a sense of the lesson framework and then invite them to talk you through what they think would be a good approach and why. This will help you gain an insight into students' perspectives on teaching and learning.

On a final note, I would direct you to my website, as well as my TES profile. At both you will find a range of free lesson-planning resources which have proved popular with teachers. These include The Starter Generator (120 starter activities), The Ultimate Lesson Activity Generator (120 main activities), and The Plenary Producer (130 plenary activities). You can access them at:

www.mikegershon.com

www.tes.co.uk/mikegershon

Chapter Six – Facilitation vs Instruction

In this chapter we will look at the two main schools of thought concerning the teacher's role in the classroom. These centre on whether the teacher should be a facilitator of learning or an instructor of students. The debate is an old one. It rests, in part, on a distinction between the two main strands of what teaching and learning is all about. First, the sense that learning ought to involve the student as the central subject. Second, that the teacher, who is in possession of superior knowledge and understanding, should be the focus.

This tension has been present in formal education since its inception. There is no definitive answer. The question is one of opinion and preference as much as evidence. The one point which we can make definitively is that the extreme of both positions is manifestly unfavourable.

A teacher who does nothing but facilitate will rob students of the opportunity to learn from their stock of knowledge and understanding. A teacher who does nothing but instruct will give their students no chance to develop an independent understanding or to practice skills effectively.

And so, with this point, does my own position become clear.

I would argue that a balance should be sought in all cases. Where that balance lies for you will depend upon your own vision of what teaching and learning should be, as well as the evidence you elicit about the progress your students make.

In the rest of this chapter I will attempt to flesh out this position by presenting an analysis of both facilitation and instruction, as well as explaining why a mixture of the two can prove preferable. By doing this, I hope to give you a framework through which you can reflect on your own teaching, your wider beliefs about what education should entail and, as a result, come to a decision about how you would like to mix these two pedagogical approaches.

What's the difference?

We begin with the obvious question. And to this we can propose a simple answer. Facilitation sees the teacher setting up situations in which students can explore ideas and information – through which they can take the lead in their own learning. Instruction sees the teacher directly instructing students as regards the learning, taking the leading role themselves and basing this on their own knowledge, understanding and experience.

One way to consider these two approaches is to return to the concept of a continuum. Here we find absolute facilitation at one end and total instruction at the other. In between are the various combinations of approach which any teacher may choose to adopt.

Using a continuum serves to characterise the debate between facilitation and instruction as a discussion about extents. To what extent should you favour one or the other? This, for me, is a more pleasing way in which to think than an either/or characterisation. Such a dualistic shaping serves to posit a false choice, predicated on the risible notion that you can only choose one or the other. This perspective, commonly seen in opinion-led pieces on the topic, ignores the lived experience of teaching.

By this I mean that teaching is a pragmatic business. We find ourselves faced with a group of students, possessed of a purpose (to maximise progress) and with a lesson plan in hand which, we hope, will allow us to square the circle.

As we teach the lesson, we respond to what happens. We adapt and change in accordance with how our students react. We make use of the range of strategies, activities and techniques we have assembled to try to achieve our purpose in light of the reality which greets us. This is why teaching is pragmatic. It is also why an either/or debate is never useful.

Outstanding teachers are not hidebound. They do not take up a position and stick to it regardless. They tend to possess guiding principles about what they think learning and teaching is or ought to involve, but they are happy to use various means in order to achieve their ends.

Thus, for example, an outstanding teacher may look at a section of the curriculum for which they need to plan a scheme of work, identify certain points at which instruction will be preferable and others where facilitation will be the best course of action. Then, when they come to teach their lessons, they will be prepared to change their minds as to this initial assessment, if the evidence in front of them warrants it.

Should you come across an either/or debate surrounding facilitation and instruction I would advise you to discount it. Choosing one side and ignoring the other will cut you off from a huge range of tools and approaches which otherwise might prove incredibly useful in helping you to achieve your purpose of maximising progress.

As with any position, venturing to the extreme will cut you off from benefits to which a more tempered view gives access.

Opting to praise facilitation at the same time as deriding instruction means your students will never have the benefit of a clear, lucid exemplification of information or ideas about which you have expert knowledge. Similarly, an outright rejection of facilitation in favour of complete instruction will remove from students the opportunity to engage with ideas on their own terms and to develop a sense of independence.

Viewed in this light, we can see why a mix and match approach is preferable. It allows the teacher to draw on the strengths visible at both ends of the continuum. At the same time, there is still room for the teacher to make a choice as to which end they prefer, with this then informing the exact percentages involved in the mix.

For example, a teacher who favours instruction but also understand the benefits of facilitation might teach lessons split roughly 70/30 in favour of the former. Whereas a teacher who feels a natural affinity for facilitation yet also recognises that without instruction major benefits are lost, might opt for a similar split travelling in the opposite direction.

All of this leads us back to the point we made in the introduction to the chapter: that it will be for you to decide where your preference lies. In so doing, you will be able to develop a pragmatic approach which both satisfies whatever preference you identify, while also taking account of the benefits which come from being open to the use of both methods.

To help you in this decision, we will now look at some of the benefits and drawbacks of each in turn.

The Benefits and Drawbacks of Facilitation

Facilitation is student-led. The teacher creates situations in which students can take the lead. This sees them controlling the learning, with this control being a result of their being the focus of the lesson, rather than the teacher. Good facilitation relies on a high level of teacher expertise. This is for two reasons. First, the teacher must be able to carefully plan a series of activities which allow students to effectively engage with the content and have their thinking challenged. Second, the teacher must spend the lesson supporting students, using various techniques such as circulating (moving through the room) and questioning to maximise engagement and tacitly direct the thinking students do.

The three greatest benefits of facilitation are as follows.

First, it encourages students to be active. By active we do not mean that students are getting up and moving around the room. Rather, we mean that they are intellectually active; closely engaged with the learning the teacher has asked them to do.

Second, it encourages the use of high-order thinking skills such as analysis, synthesis and evaluation. This is because students need to interact with whatever material has been presented to achieve the goals set out by the teacher. Put another way, they need to complete the activities. With this said, easy or weak activities will make it much harder for students to successfully engage in higher-order thinking.

Third, the teacher is in a position to use their time effectively. This is because students are focussed on the learning, rather than the teacher. Thus, the teacher does not need to remain at the front of the class and attempt to hold everybody's attention. Instead, they can move through the room and support students as and when appropriate. As they do this they elicit information about students' knowledge and understanding, using this to inform the interventions they make. Clearly, this gives rise to more accurate and more efficient teaching and learning than would otherwise be the case.

On the flipside, we have the three greatest drawbacks of facilitation.

First, poorly constructed facilitation lessons stymie students' opportunities to make progress. For example, if the teacher proposes a series of activities which are too easy for the learners, then disengagement will set in. For this reason, activities need to be carefully designed to ensure students face a continued degree of challenge as they work through the material presented to them. In addition, consideration needs to be given to where the class as a whole are currently at and where different groups of students are at. Doing this means the teacher can shape their planning more carefully to ensure it engages and meets the needs of all students, rather than just some.

Second, not all students respond positively to being asked to lead their own learning. Some may find the task difficult. Others may not like the idea of having to take control. And some may feel they are being short-changed, turning to the teacher in expectation that the information be presented by them, as in the traditional model.

Third, there are times when facilitation is either inappropriate or counter-productive. Students need to be told certain things, or simply need to know whether a particular thing is right or wrong. In maths, for example, the teacher tends to need to show students how a certain operation works before they can go on and apply it themselves. Another example comes from English, where direct instruction on punctuation rules prior to active practice is generally preferable to an activity in which students have to do all of the work by themselves.

These drawbacks illustrate the point that facilitation as an approach tends to run into problems when it is not used sufficiently carefully or when there is content or material which students are required to learn off-by-heart. In the first case, the method loses its efficacy. In the second case, the benefits of the method are far less pronounced and, indeed, pale in comparison to the benefits offered by instruction.

Facilitation is therefore a fantastic approach in certain situations, most notably those when there is much to be gained from giving students the opportunity to take the lead. It can be misused but, with practice and attention to detail, will frequently lead to excellent outcomes. It is often a highly efficient approach, freeing up the teacher's time and allowing them to be more effective. Yet it does also require the teacher to do a certain amount of training, or provide a certain level of guidance, to ensure all students can access the benefits it brings.

Briefly developing the last point, we can note that those students for whom facilitation might be a turn-off can usually be brought round if the teacher either trains them in how to lead their own learning (giving them the tools they initially lack) or breaks down what they need to do into a series of steps (making the cognitive work expected of them easier to achieve).

In conclusion, outstanding facilitation involves an awareness of the benefits and drawbacks of the approach. A teacher familiar with these will be able to play up and take advantage of the former while mitigating or avoiding the latter.

The Benefits and Drawbacks of Instruction

We move now to instruction, which is teacher-led. Here, the teacher is the focus. They present students with information and ideas. Learning is the result. But this learning takes place through students paying attention to the teacher, the things they say and the things they ask students to do and think about as a result of their instruction.

Excellent instruction requires a high level of teacher expertise. This expertise covers two categories. First is knowledge and understanding. In order to instruct students effectively, the teacher must be confident and secure in the topics about which they are teaching. If not, they risk communicating ambiguously or passing on information which is partial or incomplete. Second is knowledge and understanding of how to engage an audience. Ineffective instruction sees students bored and disengaged. In such situations, the benefit of being given access to the teacher's subject expertise is lost because students are simply not attending to what is being conveyed. Techniques such as story-telling, using examples, giving opportunities to discuss and reflect on the ideas enumerated and making use of different media formats to supplement speech all come into play here.

The three greatest benefits of instruction are as follows.

First, the teacher knows and understands more than their students. Through instruction they can give students direct access to this, helping them to learn more quickly than might otherwise be the case. Of particular note are the ways in which teachers can demonstrate meaning, connections, uses, evaluation points and other such aspects that it would take students a long time to grasp if they were doing all the work themselves.

Second, through instruction the teacher can show students the correct way to do certain processes or procedures. So too can they demonstrate one or more skilful ways in which to think about a given topic (here I am acknowledging that in many cases there is more than one 'correct' way of thinking about something). This is modelling – one of the most powerful teaching techniques. Modelling encompasses physical demonstrations, verbal exemplification, the use of exemplar work and the teaching of thinking (i.e. the modelling of thinking processes).

Third, the teacher can explicitly address, explain and correct common misconceptions connected to the topic of study. This helps students avoid such misconceptions as well as to appreciate their origins. The teacher is in a position to direct students' thinking and help them understand why they may be inclined to think in a certain way, even though this may not be correct.

On the flipside, we have the three greatest drawbacks of instruction.

First, students may become and then remain passive. By passive I mean that are not actively engaged with the learning. Rather than attending directly to the instruction provided by the teacher, they let it wash over them. This usually arises for one of two reasons. First, the teacher falls into the trap of assuming the mind is a bucket. They pour forth information, expecting that this will fall into students' minds and, as a result, be known and understood. Second, the teacher may fail to appreciate that intellectual activity needs to be stimulated and encouraged. Such a failure sees instruction of the dreary lecture type, in which an hour of unexpurgated prose gushes from the teacher's mouth without any thought given to how this could be broken up or studded with opportunities for students to think actively about what is being said.

Second, instruction is not allied with the opportunity for practice. Practice allows for the development of understanding and the refinement of skill. Without it, learning is unlikely to become embedded. Nor is mastery likely to flow forth. A lesson in which the teacher only instructs is a lesson in which students are unable to do much with the information to which they are being given access. It is in the doing that one is able to come to terms, process and assess. Through this, new information is unpicked, analysed and compared to that which one already knows. Thus, instruction without practice is simply telling – and telling alone is not a hugely effective method of teaching.

Third, instruction is seen as a get out clause for teacher and students. When this situation arises it is usually because a tacit understanding has developed between teacher and students which runs something like this: if I am standing at the front of the class instructing, and you are sitting down listening, we won't have any problems and we can all assume that learning is going on. Such an understanding makes life easy for teacher and students. No one has to put in much effort yet everyone can say that they have done their job. It evokes a degree of mediocrity and complacency akin to the facilitative teacher who sets up an activity and leaves students to get on with things, happy in the belief that hustle and bustle is itself an indication of learning.

These drawbacks illustrate the point that instruction is rarely effective on its own. It always needs to be allied to some element of practice, or the teacher needs to give thought to when and how students will be able to actively engage with what the instruction encompasses. The key is to avoid the enticing yet false proposition that the simple act of instructing is enough. It is not. This is true in all realms of teaching, not just the classroom.

Take the driving instructor, for example. They instruct the learner on how to drive, showing and telling them what is necessary, but, at the same time, the learner has ample opportunity to actively engage with this information by trying to drive the car.

Similarly, the football manager who instructs their players on how they want them to defend does not then leave it at that. Instead they provide plenty of opportunities for the players to put the instructions into practice, prior to the next match.

Using Progress as a Yardstick

You will see from the two previous sections that I have sought to present a balanced view of instruction and facilitation, outlining the positive and negative aspects of each. This has been done in part to give you a neutral overview of each approach and in part to further the argument I made at the start of the chapter that a mix of both methods is preferable.

But how do we come to decide on the make-up of that mix? Is there a means through which we can try to make good judgements about how much facilitation and how much instruction we include in our lessons?

Well, perhaps there is.

If we accept, as has been proposed elsewhere in the book, that progress is our purpose and that progress means the maximisation of learning, then maybe we can use this as the yardstick by which to judge how much facilitation and how much instruction we include in any particular lesson.

The question then becomes: What mixture will help ensure the most progress possible?

Granted, you will not be able to answer this question with complete accuracy right away. The more experience you get through the course of your training year and beyond, the better placed you will be to answer it. However, even at the very start of your training, you will be in a position to develop a reasoned response, based on a consideration of what your lesson is about and where you want students to be by the end of it.

Let us look at an example to show how this might work.

We are planning a lesson on human rights for a Year 10 Citizenship class. By the end of the lesson, we want students to be able to explain what human rights are, give their opinion on whether everyone should be entitled to them and assess the strengths and weaknesses of protecting them through the law.

From here, we can to begin to think about how we will mix facilitation and instruction.

First, we note that students may not be completely familiar with the concept and history of human rights. This, therefore, may lend itself to instruction. Next, we note that to form an opinion students will need to engage with the material from their own perspective and, ideally, will also need to be exposed to other perspectives. This tends towards facilitation. Finally, we can see that to assess the strengths and weaknesses, students will probably need some initial guidance (for example, the modelling of a thinking process) before engaging with the work on their own or in groups.

Thus, in this case, by quickly analysing where we want students to be at the end of our lesson, we find ourselves in a position to say that we will aim for roughly 60% facilitation and 40% instruction. The approaches will be applied in the lesson segments we plan, each of which will tie to the aims we outlined above.

This example illustrates how the general sense of using progress as a yardstick can be contextualised in individual lessons. To do so, we identify what we expect progress to look like – what we want students to know or be able to do by the end of the lesson – and work backwards from there, identifying whether facilitation or instruction is a better option at any given point.

In most cases, this will lead us to a mixture. As seen in the example, and as we have been saying throughout, it is unlikely a complete focus on facilitation or instruction will yield the maximum amount of progress. Therefore, relying too much on one or the other risks preventing students from learning as much as they might.

Mixing Facilitation and Instruction

Here I would like to provide you with some further practical examples of how facilitation and instruction can be mixed. The purpose is to give you some ideas you can apply in your own lessons, helping you to broaden your experience and giving you the chance to reflect on the kind of learning to which these examples lead.

Instruction – Facilitation – Reflection:

This model sees the teacher instructing students on a topic before giving them the opportunity to lead their own learning, based on what has initially been said. Finally, there is a reflection in which the results of the instruction and the facilitation are tied together.

So, for example, the teacher may begin by explaining to students the three most common designs for bridges, including an analysis of the thinking involved and the reasons for their continued use. They may then set up an activity in which students have to create their own bridges using a selection of disparate materials. Finally, the teacher would lead a reflection in which they help students to think about how easy it was to apply the information they received at the start of the lesson to their own building projects and what they learned as a result of this endeavour.

Facilitation – Instruction – Reflection:

Here the previous model is reversed. The aim is to immerse students in the topic straight away, engaging them and encouraging active learning. After this, the teacher instructs students in order to codify what they have discovered and address any misconceptions.

Using the example from above, we would begin by presenting students with the materials and inviting them to construct one or more different types of bridge. After this, we would instruct them on the most common types, connecting this to what they produced themselves. The reflection would then focus on how students set about developing their ideas and how this relates to the best practice subsequently explained by the teacher.

Discussion – Lecture – Active Practice – Teacher Talk – Repeated Practice:

Students enter the room and find a discussion question connecting a new topic to their prior experience. The teacher invites them to discuss this in pairs. After the discussion, the teacher provides a short lecture, introducing the new topic and situating it in the context of students' prior knowledge. They then present an activity in which students are to practice using the key ideas introduced by the teacher.

While this activity takes place, the teacher circulates through the room, observing and listening. They then draw the class back together and explain what they have seen and heard. As part of this, they make suggestions and provide models as to how students can improve what they are doing. The activity then resumes, except this time students are challenging themselves to employ the guidance the teacher has just provided.

Activity – Activity – Activity – Teacher-led Plenary:

This model falls more heavily on the side of facilitation. The teacher plans a series of three activities, each more challenging than the last, through which students will be leading their own learning. For example, we might have a first activity in which students have to read and then discuss a series of sources connected to the topic. Next, students would be asked to produce a report focussing on the accuracy and reliability of the sources. Finally, students would need to offer an interpretation of the topic based on the information they have been able to glean from the sources.

After this, the emphasis moves back to instruction. The teacher leads a plenary in which they talk students through an analysis and evaluation of the sources. As they do this, students are expected to reflect on and think about how they conducted their investigations and to what extent they met the standards demonstrated by the teacher.

Teacher Talk – Activity – Teacher Talk – Activity:

A classic model seen in many classrooms the world over. The lesson begins with the teacher talking students through information and/or ideas relevant to the topic. An activity is then introduced which gives students the opportunity to apply that which the teacher has explained. During the activity, the teacher circulates, asking questions, providing further modelling and addressing misconceptions.

When the time is up, the teacher presents new information or ideas. This material is more challenging than that which came first. A second activity is then introduced. Students engage with this while the teacher again circulates, with the intention of pushing thinking and supporting those who might be struggling with the more demanding content.

These five models can be adapted to any subject and any age-group. Each has its benefits, implicit in the explanations I have provided. Play around with them as part of your lesson planning and see how they feel to teach. Critically reflect on your experiences and you will be well on your way to developing a sound sense of when and where to favour instruction over facilitation and vice versa.

Building a Repertoire

Our concluding thoughts bring us to the idea of building a repertoire. To be an outstanding trainee teacher, you need to be able to demonstrate the ability to plan and teach lessons which effectively meet the needs of the students in front of you. As we mentioned at the start of the chapter, this involves the cultivation of a pragmatic attitude. One which welcomes both facilitation and instruction as methods possessed of benefits, but also acknowledges the limitations inherent in each and, by extension, the danger of privileging one and ignoring the other.

As you will note from the previous section, many different mixtures of facilitation and instruction are possible. There is no universal optimum appropriate for all situations. The key is to look at what you want your students to achieve and to then make your decisions accordingly.

Through the course of your training, pay attention to the effects wrought by your use of facilitation and instruction. Be critical. Even if you lean toward one method, it is important you retain objectivity when analysing whether its use led to what you hoped for or not.

Thinking in this way helps you to become more discriminatory. You will be better placed to decide what type of approach – what mixture – will yield the best results. In addition, your repertoire will develop at a significant pace. This is because you will be paying attention to the activities you use, meaning analysis and evaluation of them will be at the forefront of your mind.

As ever, your progress can be further speeded up by observing others and reflecting on the approaches they take – including the results engendered. In most schools you will find colleagues who favour instruction and those who prefer facilitation. Observing these teachers will open up a range of ideas which you can take away and make your own, helping you to develop your repertoire.

Finally, it is worth seeing your training year as a formative experience when it comes to facilitation and instruction; an experience which will be all the better if you try different things and, in so doing, seek to learn from your mistakes. Most people who enter the profession do so with an often unrealised bias towards either facilitation or instruction. Challenging this bias by trying out different approaches during your training makes you a more rounded teacher. It also helps you to critically reflect on what you believe to be the best way to make learning happen. Whether this results in a change of mind or not is a moot point. The important thing is that you end up with more experience on which to base your decisions and, as a consequence, a wider repertoire of skills on which to call.

All that remains is for me to present some questions and activities to help you in this processes of reflection, trial and error and pedagogical development.

Questions

- To what extent do you feel comfortable standing in front of the class and imparting knowledge to your students? Do your comfort levels vary depending on the topic you are teaching?

- To what extent do you feel comfortable letting students lead their own learning? Do you think you could keep everybody's focus on learning if you were not stood at the front of the class, holding everyone's attention?

- Do you agree with my characterisation of the differences between facilitation and instruction, including their relative strengths and weaknesses? Why?

- Should teachers take account of students' preferences when deciding how to mix facilitation and instruction in a lesson?

- Which teaching method did you favour when you were at school? Did this method cause you to learn the most? Why?

Activities

- Choose a topic and plan two imaginary lessons. In the first, your focus should be completely on facilitation. In the second you should look only at instruction. Compare the lessons you create and walk through them from the perspective of a student. What would they be like? What learning would happen? What would be missed?

- If you are in a position where you can teach the same lesson twice (to two different classes) do so, but vary the mix of facilitation and instruction on each occasion. While teaching, analyse how students respond. Afterwards, compare the results of the two lessons. Think about the learning which took place, the atmosphere, your role and the experience the students had.

- Create a continuum on a sheet of A3 paper. Label one end as facilitation and one end as instruction. As you plan and teach more lessons, fill in the continuum by making brief entries detailing different activities you use.

This will help you to get a sense of which approach you favour and whether you need to work on developing a degree of balance. It is also a useful aide memoire for future planning.

Chapter Seven – Sustaining Pace and Challenge

At this point, a moment's reflection will serve us well.

We are pursuing our aim of being an outstanding trainee teacher. To begin, we looked at the nature of teaching and learning, helping us to develop a critical understanding of both. Then, we thought about what it means to be a teacher, before going on to examine how we can best understand our learners. From there, we turned our attention to planning lessons, gaining an insight into the mechanics of the task and how we can both speed up the process and maximise progress. Then, in the last chapter, we sought to unpick the competing perspectives on how a teacher should teach. In so doing, we demonstrated the merit in each approach, as well as the benefits which accrue from mixing the two.

Here, we will continue to build on everything we have done so far. Our aim is simple. To provide a practical insight into how to sustain pace and challenge. Therefore, the chapter can be thought of us a direct companion to the previous two which, taken together, help to form the foundations of planning and teaching lessons in which learning is central and students' progress is pushed as far as possible.

This will be a highly practical chapter, perhaps the most practical yet, offering a range of techniques and strategies you can try out through the course of your training. As ever, remember the benefits which come from trial and error. The mistakes you make when trying out new ideas are always fruitful. They show you how to progress and develop, giving you information you can use to become an ever-improving teacher and, hopefully fairly quickly, an outstanding one.

Differentiation

There is a lot of confusion over what differentiation is. The term has become unnecessarily vague. Put simply, differentiation means all the things the teacher does to help students make progress, regardless of their starting points.

It is synonymous with personalisation (a term which was recently popular but whose use is now less common). This is because to personalise a lesson means to help different students access the learning and achieve well. This is the same as securing progress across the board.

By differentiating effectively, you can sustain pace and challenge. This is because you will be doing things which help all learners to access the work. This minimises disengagement, generates a sense of purpose and allows you to challenge all learners (because, having accessed the work, they are now in a position to have their thinking challenged).

A useful way to think about differentiation is to divide it into five categories:

- Questioning

- Activities

- Words and writing

- Things the teacher can do or use

- Things students can do or use

Thinking in this way gives purchase. The concept is no longer large and unwieldy. Instead, it becomes specific and tied to practical classroom experience.

If you are ever uncertain whether you are differentiating sufficiently, ask yourself whether every student in the class is in a position to access the learning and make progress. If they are not, think about the five categories and identify one thing you could do straight away to help improve matters. When you have done this, return to the categories and see if there is something else you could do. Working in this way helps you to create and teach lessons which are highly personalised and take account of the relative needs of most if not all learners.

A few examples then, to contextualise the categories.

Questioning is self-explanatory. Every time we ask a question to a student, to a pair or to a group, we are in a position to differentiate. This is because we can tailor our questions to the student or students to whom they are posed. So, for example, we might ask a student who appears to be struggling a series of questions which help them to think about how the lesson content connects to what they already know. Or, we might simply ask them what is wrong and what help they would like.

Activities is another straightforward category. It encompasses all the activities you plan. Differentiated activities allow students to engage with the content at their own level. This could be through the provision of choices or options, sub-tasks, extension tasks, group work or the use of discussion to underpin written answers (the former being an easier means through to articulate, edit and refine thoughts than the latter).

Words and writing covers all literacy matters. That is, speaking, listening, reading and writing. Tools to support less-able students include sentence starters, writing frames, exemplar sentences or paragraphs and images which supplement written or verbal definitions. More-able students can be challenged to write or read more complex pieces of work, to speak and listen in accordance with certain criteria, or to take on different perspectives when engaging in any of these activities.

Things the teacher can do or use covers modelling, talking, circulating, intervening, explaining and the like. You will also note that questioning could fit in here. This demonstrates the fact that, while the categories are a useful tool through which to think, they are not mutually exclusive. Talking to students is always a good way to differentiate. If you talk to most of your class during the course of a lesson, you can be sure that you have helped them to engage with the learning at their own level.

Finally, we have things students can do or use. This includes the obvious, such as dictionaries and thesauruses, as well as the less obvious such as scrap paper (to store information and thus free up short-term memory), mnemonic devices, working with peers, exemplar work and asking questions. In all these cases, the aim is either to give students a tool which extends their capacity to think and act, or to present a method which allows them to further their knowledge and understanding.

Returning to these categories when planning and teaching lessons ensures you are always doing things which help all students to access the learning. This means your teaching will always involve a high level of differentiation.

Next we go on to look at specific things you can do to challenge the thinking of different groups of students. These strategies will stretch their thinking at the same time as they maintain the pace of your lessons.

Challenging Less-Able Students

Characteristically, less-able students struggle to deal with abstract thought. This does not mean they cannot access this type of thought, just that to do so is often, at first, a challenge. As such, a good way to challenge less-able students is to ask questions or set tasks which straddle the concrete and the abstract.

For example, in a geography lesson we might give these students a list of pull factors and push factors connected to migration, with each one being explained by an imaginary figure (Reza decided to move to Europe because he thought he could get a better education there). We could then ask students to sort these into the two groups of push and pull before ranking the items in each group from most to least influential. Finally, we could challenge students to write a short, evaluative summary explaining whether they believe migration tends to be a result of push factors, pull factors or a combination of the two.

This example demonstrates how a carefully planned activity can move from the concrete (individuals giving reasons for their migration) to the abstract (deciding whether, in general, push or pull factors are more significant). Not only does such an approach challenge less-able students, but it does so in a progressive way, increasing the chance they will be able to successfully meet that challenge.

This method can be applied across the board and with different age groups. Simply bear in mind the gradual movement from concrete to abstract thought when planning an activity or the application of an activity to your less-able students' attempts to learn.

Challenging Middle Ability Students

Middle ability students are often overlooked. This means their thinking isn't challenged and that, for them, the lesson lacks pace.

This usually happens because teachers spend time attending to the less-able and more-able students, hoping the main body of the lesson will be sufficient to push those in the middle. But this can only be the case if we think in advance about how this plays out in practice.

Fortunately, there are two simple techniques you can employ to ensure middle ability learners are always challenged in your lessons.

The first is to make it clear that any work you set for more-able students is presented as being a challenge for all students. This sees you encouraging the more-able students to engage with such work but also making it clear that middle ability students can take to it as well. In part, this is about communicating high expectations and reinforcing these on a regular basis. For example, you might reveal a pair of extension questions specifically designed to challenge the more-able (who you suspect will definitely get onto them) but then, as the lesson progresses, you would also direct middle ability students to these as they progress through the main body of work.

The second is to introduce added levels of complexity to activities mid-way through. For example, imagine we have a PE class who are practising long and short passing in football. We might spend our time working with the less-able students while the middle ability and more-able hone their skills. About halfway through the activity, we would introduce two or three caveats such as:

- You must change feet with every pass you make

- You must alternate between ground passes and passes through the air

- You must use the outside of your foot to make your pass

We would then indicate that students should choose which caveat they will work to apply, or which two they will take on.

This neatly covers middle ability and more-able students, challenging both.

The former can select one of the caveats and practise this until it is perfected, while the latter can choose two of the caveats and attempt to master both at the same time.

Again, you can adapt these methods to fit with whatever subject and whichever age-group you are teaching.

Challenging More-Able Students

When it comes to challenging more-able students, it is vital that we don't fall into the trap of simply giving them more of the same to do. Not only is this boring for them, it isn't actually challenging either. If they have completed a task or mastered a skill, asking them to do more of the same will neither push them nor stretch them. This means progress will not be maximised.

So we need to plan to make greater demands of our more-able students.

A simple technique, shown to support all learners involved, is peer teaching. If a more-able student completes the work you have set, invite them to teach one or more of their peers. The process of teaching sees the student in question having to go back over their learning, analyse it and then synthesise it so as to present it in a way which aids the understanding of whomever they are teaching.

Two points to note before we look at another technique. It is best to provide some guidance so students do not feel you are simply lumbering them with an unwanted task. First, specify who you want the student in question to support. This could be an individual, a group, or a set of students all struggling with the same issue. Second, give clear instructions as to what the teaching should entail. For example: 'Can you help Johnny to develop his answers. He's struggling to think of more than one reason. Talk him through the different reasons and give him examples of why they are appropriate.' Here, the challenge is specific and personalised. This leads to better outcomes and is more motivating.

A second useful technique involves asking students to construct or predict possible questions (or tasks) which could be used to test someone's learning about the topic of study. This process sees students having to take a general view of the content, before focussing in on specifics. They then have to take this and construct questions suitable for eliciting the information necessary to see what learning has taken place, which is challenging.

As with the previous two sections, both techniques here explained can be adapted for use across the board.

Using Questioning to Challenge All Students

We now turn to look at questioning in a little more depth. First we will think about how to challenge all students, then about individual cases.

Good questions should provoke thinking. Sometimes this thinking will need to be fairly heavily circumscribed – such as when we are checking knowledge or testing whether a student can apply an idea in a certain way. However, as a rule, challenging questions are more open than this. They afford multiple answers and rely on a degree of reasoning, creativity or critical thinking from the student.

This means they provoke thinking of a more complex, and therefore challenging, type. With this in mind, here are three simple ways you can ask challenging questions to all the students you teach:

Big Question to Frame the Lesson: Instead of using a title as the basis of your lesson, use a question. Make this a big question and explain to students that, through the course of the lesson, your shared aim is to try to answer this. Immediately, the lesson becomes more challenging, especially if you spend a little time attending to your question, making sure it is sufficiently big and engaging. As the lesson progresses, you can regularly return to the question to see how close students are to being able to answer it.

Conceptual Questions: Base questions around concepts. These are abstract ideas, such as change, right and wrong, or reliability, and therefore challenging to think about. Every area of the curriculum has a guiding set of concepts. It is to these that specific content is attached. Identify concepts relevant for the subject and/or age group you teach and use these as the basis for challenging questions.

Provisional Questions: Inserting the word 'might' into a question serves to make knowledge provisional. Thus, 'What is the answer?' becomes, 'What might the answer be?' Clearly, the second question is more stimulating than the first. This is because it provokes speculation, reasoning and justification in a way that the first doesn't. Asking questions of this type – making them a norm in your lessons – helps to continually challenge all students and keep up the pace in your lessons.

Using Questions to Challenge Individual Students

We can also tailor our questioning so it challenges individual students. This means we ask specific students specific questions predicated on their prior knowledge and understanding. The high degree of precision engendered by such an approach leads to questions which push students to think more deeply than would otherwise be the case.

This can be seen through a brief comparison. In situation one we walk around the room and ask the same question to three different students, eliciting three responses of varying quality. In situation two, we walk around the room and ask three different questions to three different students, each one informed by what we know about their current level of knowledge and understanding.

The second approach produces higher quality answers and challenges students far more than the first approach.

Here are three techniques you can use to help tailor your questions to individual students:

Observe/Listen then Question: During an activity, circulate through the room. Identify a student who will benefit from having their thinking stretched. Observe them working, observe their work or listen to the conversations they are having with other students. Use this information to inform the questions you pose. This allows you to ask questions which are appropriate, challenging and personalised. Students will also be in a position to immediately respond because your question will connect to their current thinking.

Mark then Question: Another way to elicit information about where students are currently at is through marking. You can either mark students' work outside lessons or, if time allows, during the lesson. In the latter case, this usually involves reading or observing the work produced by one or more students. In either case, having marked (assessed) the work which has been produced, you are then in an excellent position from which to ask a relevant, challenging question. This could be done verbally, if you are in the lesson. Or, if you are marking work outside the lesson, it could be written in a student's book. If it is the latter, ensure you give students an opportunity to write a response.

Opinion, Counter, Defend: Here we select a student who is engaged in the activity and ask them to share their thoughts or opinions concerning the work they are doing. Having listened carefully we then pose a counter-point. This could be an alternative explanation, a different perspective, a different way of working or something else entirely. The aim is to challenge whatever the student has put forward. Having done this, we then look to the student to defend their original position. This is challenging and should provoke the beginning of an evaluative to and fro between you and the student in question.

Bloom's Taxonomy

We move now to consider an exceptionally valuable tool all teachers can call on to ensure their lessons retain good pace and a high level of challenge. That tool is Bloom's Taxonomy of Educational Objectives.

The taxonomy was put together in the 1950s by a group of American educators led by Benjamin S. Bloom. Hence the name.

The taxonomy arranges the key cognitive processes which constitute learning from the most simple to the most complex. This serves to present us with a hierarchy of processes which, when worked through, allow an individual to gain mastery over a given topic.

The six categories are knowledge, comprehension, application, analysis, synthesis and evaluation. Subsequent research has suggested the last two categories should be swapped over. This is not of great concern to us. It is perhaps easiest to think of the categories as pairs. At the bottom of the taxonomy we have knowledge and comprehension, the two simplest processes. Next we have application and analysis, both of which are more intellectually demanding. And finally, we have synthesis and evaluation, the two processes which make the greatest cognitive demands.

Roughly speaking, a student will need to exhibit mastery in one level or pair of levels before being able to exhibit mastery at the next stage.

So, for example, you would need to know what an adjective is before you can analyse an author's use of adjectives in a piece of writing. Similarly, you would need to be able to apply the idea of political authority before you could evaluate the extent to which William Gladstone was able to maintain this during the course of his last stint as prime minister.

The model remains in use today because the delineations and ordering of thought processes it made clear are not context-dependent. Thus, while we are more than half a century further on than the educational forefathers who constructed the taxonomy, the nature of thought has not shifted a great deal during that time. We still need to know what a thing means before we can comprehend it, just as we still need to be able to analyse the use of something before we can start to create an alternative approach ourselves.

To further reinforce the point, a cursory glance at any mark-scheme provided by an exam board will reveal the taxonomy underpinning the assessment objectives. In addition, nearly all assessments and mark-schemes created in school also rest on the same structure.

We can use the taxonomy in all manner of ways to help ensure our lessons remain challenging and are imbued with good pace. It can act as the basis for lesson objectives and lesson/learning outcomes. We can use it to develop thought-provoking questions, to plan a series of progressively challenging questions (moving up the levels of the taxonomy), and to tailor our questions to specific learners (matching their current levels of understanding to different levels of the taxonomy).

We can also use the taxonomy when constructing activities. It is to this we will now turn.

Using Bloom's Taxonomy to Create Challenging Activities

The taxonomy is concerned with mastery learning. As a student progresses up the different levels, so they gain an increasing mastery of the content about which they are learning.

Here are three ways we can use this fact to create challenging activities:

Three Activities, Three Categories: In the chapter on lesson planning we suggested that a common, and highly valued approach, involves the construction of a lesson containing a starter activity, two or three main activities and a plenary. Let us take this method and say the starter activity and the main activities can be based on different levels of the taxonomy. We might even use the pairing procedure I outlined above. So, for example, our starter will focus on knowledge and comprehension, our first activity will deal with application and analysis, and our second one will look at synthesis and evaluation. Planning in this way, we can be certain that the lesson will get progressively more challenging. The taxonomy ensures it.

One Activity, Subdivided: Another approach is to take one of our main activities and to subdivide it into a series of steps, with each step based on a different level of the taxonomy. So, for example, we might have a fairly lengthy activity involving five separate steps. The first would focus on comprehension, the second on application and so on. Here, we are building a sense of challenge and progression into an individual activity. It will not necessarily be the case that all students will complete all steps. But what we can be certain of is that all students will be challenged, because they will continue to gain a mastery of the content as they progress through the steps at their own pace.

One Activity, Three Sections: This is a variation on the previous example. Instead of subdividing an activity into a series of five steps, which on some occasions can be too time-consuming, we can create an activity which has three separate sections. Here is an example of what this might look like:

Read through the information about Jewish festivals and summarise the key points in your own words **(comprehension)**. Then, compare what you have identified with your knowledge of Hindu festivals from last term – compare and contrast them to look for similarities and differences **(analysis)**. Finally, use your knowledge of Jewish and Hindu festivals to assess whether or not they are primarily about strengthening family and community bonds, or giving individuals an opportunity to display and renew their faith **(evaluation).**

As you can see, the task is inherently challenging due to the fact that it is constructed on the back of the taxonomy. When using tasks of this type, be aware that they may take longer to complete than other activities because they contain three separate elements. In addition, decide in advance whether you want all students to complete all sections, or if you will be happy for students to get as far as they can within the time you set.

Here is a selection of keywords connected to each of the levels of the taxonomy. You can use these to help you apply the taxonomy to your lesson planning:

Knowledge:
Arrange, Define, Describe, List, Match, Memorise, Name, Order, Quote, Recognise, Recall, Repeat, Reproduce, Restate, Retain.

Comprehension:
Characterise, Classify, Complete, Describe, Discuss, Establish, Explain, Express, Identify, Illustrate, Recognise, Report, Relate, Sort, Translate.

Application:
Apply, Calculate, Choose, Demonstrate, Dramatize, Employ, Implement, Interpret, Operate, Perform, Practise, Role-Play, Sketch, Solve, Suggest.

Analysis:
Analyse, Appraise, Categorize, Compare, Contrast, Differentiate, Discriminate, Distinguish, Examine, Experiment, Explore, Investigate, Question, Research, Test.

Synthesis:
Combine, Compose, Construct, Create, Devise, Design, Formulate, Hypothesise, Integrate, Merge, Organise, Plan, Propose, Synthesise, Unite.

Evaluation:
Appraise, Argue, Assess, Critique, Defend, Evaluate, Examine, Grade, Inspect, Judge, Justify, Rank, Rate, Review, Value.

Using Bloom's Taxonomy to Create Pace

Throughout this chapter we have thought of pace and challenge as going hand-in-hand. While this is true, it has meant that we haven't attended to the former quite as much as the latter. Our final two sections will correct this bias. First we will look at how we can use the taxonomy to create pace, then I will present five simple techniques on which you can call in any lesson.

Questions Framing Activities: Earlier, we noted that replacing the lesson title with a big question is an excellent means through to generate challenge. We can also create pace by framing each activity we plan with a question based on an appropriate level of Bloom's Taxonomy. This gives each lesson segment a driving purpose: to answer the question which has been posed. In addition, it creates a sense of overarching pace if we ensure that those individual questions move up the taxonomy, immediately situating each new activity as more challenging than the last.

Whole-Class Challenge Questions: If the pace of your lesson sags, ask yourself if this is because the work you have asked students to do is too easy. If it is, take your mind to the top two levels of Bloom's Taxonomy and quickly construct a question connected to the topic with which you can challenge the whole class. This technique allows you to change the focus of the lesson and, in so doing, alter the pace.

Bloom's-Based Extension Boxes: Get two shoe boxes and paint each one a different colour. One box will be the synthesis or creative thinking box. The other will be the evaluation or critical thinking box. Fill each up with a collection of extension questions and tasks. You can use the keywords listed above as the basis for these. Then, introduce the boxes to your students. Explain they will be available during every lesson and that, as soon as students complete an activity to your satisfaction, they will be able to go and choose an extension at random from either of the two boxes.

Once the system is embedded as a norm, this creates a sense of pace and drive. It has particular impact when a handful of students start to finish the main body of work and then go to select an extension. Their peers will look on enviously and work harder to achieve the goal themselves!

Five Simple Ways to Sustain Pace

As promised, here we have five techniques you can apply in almost any lesson to help sustain a good level of pace:

Time Limits and Countdowns: Setting time limits creates a sense of urgency. Depending on the age of your students, you may need to give them continued guidance on how long is left. Do be careful to ensure your time limits are realistic. If they are too short the sense of pace will be lost. The time will be up and students will not be close to finishing the work you set them! Countdowns differ slightly in that the time limit is only introduced at the end of the activity. For example, we might tell students they have two minutes left and then display an appropriate timer on the board which counts down the remaining seconds.

Circulating: During activities, circulate through the room and, as part of your efforts, remind students how much time there is available, push them to work quicker and make interventions which either speed up their work or create a greater sense of dynamism. Depending on your students, this might involve targeting the whole class, or specific individuals/groups.

Introducing New Elements: Having set students off on an activity, introduce new elements which they have to complete as well. This creates a sense of pace as you are altering the demands under which students are working. For example, you might set students off on a paired discussion task and then, halfway through the activity, introduce a subsidiary task requiring each pair to create a six-sentence summary of their discussion. In this example, the pace of work would immediately jump as students have to readjust to complete the new task in the remaining time.

Mid-Lesson Reviews: This involves taking a break during the course of the lesson to review the learning up to that point. It is also known as a mini-plenary. The review should last a couple of minutes and be led by the teacher. You can guide students in reviewing the aim of the lesson and the learning which has taken place so far. Then, you can ask students to predict what they think will happen next and why. This helps to re-energise the class, who return to their work with a renewed sense of purpose.

Big Question Track-Back: If you framed your lesson with a big question, you can continually track-back to this during the course of the session. This sees you asking students to what extent they can answer the question as well as whether or not their answers (or understanding of the question) have altered at all, based on the learning they have done. As with mid-lesson reviews, the technique is a good means through which to renew the sense of purpose underpinning the learning.

And with that, we draw our exploration of how to sustain pace and challenge to a close. It goes without saying that, in order to be an outstanding trainee teacher, you should aim to maintain a good level of pace and a high degree of challenge in every lesson you teach. Applying, practising and modifying the ideas outlined above should allow you to do just that.

We conclude, as ever, with some questions and activities designed to help you reflect on the topic and to further challenge(!) your thinking.

Questions

- Is having your thinking challenged always a comfortable experience? What might be the implications of this for teaching and learning?

- How could you train students to respond positively to challenges? Can you train students to embrace them? How?

- Is it possible to judge the pace of a lesson from your lesson plan, or is pace something you can only assess 'in the moment?'

- What characterises a lesson with good pace? How does it differ from a lesson in which the pace is too slow or too quick?

- During your time in education, when was your thinking challenged the most? What caused this, how did it feel and how did you develop as a result?

Activities

- Research Bloom's Taxonomy of Educational Objectives. There is plenty of useful information available online. You might also like to look at my free resource 'The Bloom Buster,' available at www.mikgershon.com

- Take two or three of your most recent lesson plans and two differently coloured highlighter pens. First, go through each plan and use one pen to highlight the points at which you think the lesson offers a sufficient level of challenge for all students. Then, take the second pen and highlight the points at which you think you could have included more challenge. Finally, reflect on what you will take from this and apply to the next lesson you plan.

- Challenge yourself to learn something new. It could be connected to your training or something else entirely. As you go through the challenge, pay attention to what the experience is like – both cognitively and emotionally (for example, do you get frustrated?). At the end of the process, consider what insights this has provided about how your students might view the challenges you set them.

Chapter Eight – Learning From Yourself; Learning From Others

You will make mistakes during your teacher training. This is inevitable. It is also a good thing! Mistakes are one of the main ways in which we learn. Much learning is concerned with a process of trial and error through which we come to understand the extent of what is possible and the appropriateness of applying certain things in certain situations.

Without mistakes and without trial and error learning is heavily circumscribed. This circumscription limits progress and prevents an individual from developing the same degree of insight and understanding as is possible when we fail, err and get things wrong.

Of course, making mistakes is not enough on its own. We must also analyse and reflect on these. If we make a mistake and then withdraw, refusing to engage with the information our mistake elicited, then we do not learn a great deal – perhaps even nothing at all.

Mistakes need to be embraced and seen in a positive light. You need to examine what they give rise to, reflect on what this means and make adjustments accordingly. In this chapter we will look at some of the techniques you can employ to do this, as well as how you can successfully maintain progress through the course of your training. We will also consider some of the ways in which you can maximise the effectiveness of learning from others.

Making Mistakes and Trial and Error

Mistakes come thick and fast in the classroom, especially when you are training. It is worth noting, however, that experienced teachers make mistakes as well. I made one last week, when I used an activity with my Year 11 class which wasn't sufficiently challenging. They quickly lost interest and I had to think on my feet, adapt the lesson and re-motivate them.

It is worth remembering that all teachers make mistakes for two reasons. First, it helps to normalise the process, allowing you to view your own errors in a more positive light. Second, it illuminates the central fact that when working with children and young people, it is impossible to get everything right, all the time. The only thing we can say for sure is that outstanding teachers learn from their mistakes, correct them swiftly and effectively, and, as a result, avoid repeating them.

During the course of your training you will have a lot to learn and a lot to think about. This will lead to you making mistakes and doing things in ways you later decide were not effective. In addition, you will spend much of the year trying things out. Testing ideas and activities to see how they work, if they work and whether or not they suit your style of teaching. Such testing and trialling will lead to errors. And it is from these that you will learn.

To be an outstanding trainee teacher then, you need to adopt a mindset in which you allow yourself to make mistakes, in which you look at those mistakes as learning opportunities, and in which you do not become overly self-critical.

Many trainee teachers who struggle to progress as much as they would like find themselves in this position because they feel uncomfortable with failure and therefore try to do everything possible to minimise the chance of making mistakes. However, this seriously diminishes their scope for development. The lessons they plan and teach tend to become mechanical and their repertoire of strategies, techniques and activities remains limited. This has the knock-on effect of restricting learning in their classrooms, meaning they do not achieve their ultimate purpose of maximising student achievement.

Throughout your training year, you should look to try things out. Testing new ideas helps you develop the quality of your teaching. It also broadens and deepens your skills base. Taking risks will not always result in perfect lessons, but it will give you information about why something is or is not successful. You can then use this information to influence your future decision-making.

We can break down the process of making and analysing mistakes into three separate areas: during lessons, after lessons and in conversation with your mentor.

During lessons, you will see first-hand and immediately the effects of making mistakes. For example, you may fail to explain something clearly, meaning students struggle to understand what you are saying. A raft of questions and quizzical looks will follow.

In these situations, two things are imperative. The first is to analyse why things have turned out other than you expected. This process of real-time reflection allows you to distinguish the key learning you can take away from the event. It also points you in the direction of what you need to do to improve matters: how you should respond to get the learning back on track.

This is the second thing you must do: respond. If you do not, the results of the mistake will not be mitigated and, crucially, you will lose the opportunity to employ a corrective and observe what impact this has (bearing in mind that it could be the wrong corrective and fail to have any impact!).

In summary, when you make mistakes in lessons, assess why you think the mistake has occurred and then trial a means of correction. As you do, assess whether this is effective. If it is not, decide whether to try something else or whether to leave matters for the moment and reflect on them in more depth later on.

After lessons you have another chance through which to learn from your mistakes. The experience of this is rather difference. Time will have passed since the mistake was made and the fraught intensity of the classroom will be far behind you. Here, you can reflect with a greater sense of detachment on what happened, why it happened and the effect of any attempted correctives.

It is worth taking some time at the end of every day to sit down and run through any lessons you taught. As you do this, focus on identifying what you can take away from these lessons and use in the future. Your emphasis should be on the positive benefits of making mistakes, not on the development of a critical or negative commentary regarding what went wrong. Such ways of thinking are an easy trap to fall into, but they represent a restraint on progress rather than a support.

Avoiding putting a negative spin on mistakes takes self-control. You must remind yourself that the greatest benefit you can derive is to take away something positive, not to swamp yourself with critical thoughts. We are not seeking to re-frame all errors through rose-tinted glasses. Simply to see them in a detached matter and to take from them whatever benefits and insights we can draw.

You will also have an opportunity to discuss your mistakes with your mentor. The efficacy of this depends to some extent on the relationship you have with them. If it is a good one, discussing mistakes will be easy. The openness which comes from a strong rapport will help the pair of you to debate errors in a spirit of positive reflection.

If your relationship with your mentor is other than you would like it to be, I would suggest seeking to take control of the discussion, directing it very clearly down the path you want it to take. So, for example, you might say something like this: 'I noticed in the lesson that, on a couple of occasions, I failed to give enough support to some of the less-able students. I'd like us to think about why this happened and what I can do next time to improve things.'

Here, we have defined the problem, demonstrated our awareness of it and set a clear and positive target for the discussion. Thus, we are in control, ensuring the time we have with our mentor is used to further our own ends (improving the quality of our teaching) as much as possible.

Setting and Implementing Targets

By reflecting on your mistakes while teaching, after teaching and in discussion with your mentor, you will provide yourself with a great deal of useful information. You will identify what is going wrong, what is causing this to happen and how you might rectify matters.

As we mentioned earlier, the key to swift development is to embrace mistakes and to seek to learn from them. This learning involves the setting and implementation of targets.

A target is a desired end we have for ourselves or for somebody else (such as when we set a student a target); it is something towards which we can aim. When we achieve our target, we know that we have made progress. We then find ourselves in a position to set a new target upon which we can focus our efforts. This process is the basis of continuous improvement.

As a rule, it is best to set yourself one target at a time. The reason for this is simple. With one target to aim for, you can devote all of your energies to its pursuit. This increases the likelihood that you will achieve your target and achieve it quickly. Multiple targets, while tempting, pull the mind in different directions and make it harder to achieve effective progression.

To illustrate the point, consider how you would feel if you were asked to improve your behaviour management, better stretch the thinking of more-able learners and ask more thoughtful questions, all at the same time.

Compare this to if you were asked to pursue only one of these targets at a time.

Your feelings, and the likelihood of success, would be far better in the second case.

The targets underpinning your progression as a trainee teacher can come from two places: your mentor or yourself (and sometimes a combination of the two, as when you and your mentor discuss and agree a target in conjunction).

Either way, you will find these targets easier to use if they follow a few simple rules. First, they should be unambiguous and specific. Second, they should be achievable. Third, they should be tied to a clear sense of what success will look like.

If you are setting yourself a target, use information gathered from your mistakes to identify something you would like to improve. Then, hone in on what it is precisely you think you need to change or develop in order to make this improvement. Having done this, ask whether what you have identified is achievable. If it is, great. If not, break it down into a series of smaller steps. Finally, work out what success will look like – in terms of outcomes, results or something else appropriate to the target.

If your mentor sets you a target, ask them to keep to the rules outlined above and, if necessary, explain why this will be to your benefit. In addition, ask them to provide you with one or more examples of what successful implementation of the target will look like. Here, you are asking them to model success for you. They may do this anyway but, if they don't, you can always ask them to provide you with the requisite exemplar from which to work.

Should you have enough time available, and should your mentor be willing, a useful process to follow is this:

- Discuss the mistakes you identified with your mentor.

- Work together to agree a target which addresses these mistakes and which you will be able to implement.

- Ask your mentor to give you examples of how to successfully implement the target. If possible, ask them to show you such an example – either in a general sense there and then, or in a specific sense as part of one of their lessons.

The great benefit of this process is that it closes the gap between the setting of the target and its implementation. It does this by giving you a clear demonstration – a model – to which you can refer when trying to put the target into practice during your own teaching and/or planning. This does not mean that you are copying the model or asking your mentor to do all the work for you. Rather, it means you are asking your mentor to exemplify what success looks like as explicitly as possible. This gives you a much higher chance of being successful – and of being able to make the changes you want as quickly as possible.

With all this said, do not be disheartened if some targets require perseverance – if you find yourself struggling to implement them effectively, even with clear modelling and support. Such is life! Sometimes our goals are a little further away than we imagined. Don't worry about it. The key is to keep applying effort in the direction specified and to keep reflecting on the results of that effort, making tweaks where necessary and asking for advice as and when appropriate.

Sometimes, it is even worth putting a target to one side for a few weeks, concentrating fully on something else, and then returning to it. This process ensures your attention is still focussed on a single target and that making progress remains at the forefront of your mind, but it also helps to unblock a path that may have become more difficult to pass along than you would like.

In conclusion, we can say two things.

First, and linking to the earlier section of this chapter, the targets you set for yourself, or which your mentor sets for you, should be based at least in part on the information you elicit through making mistakes and engaging in trial and error while teaching and planning. Second, continually setting and then working towards these precise, specific targets will help you to make significant progress throughout the course of the year.

Effective Self-Reflection

Within everything we have said so far, there has been an implicit recognition that effective self-reflection is an inherent aspect of becoming an outstanding trainee teacher. This has been couched in the terms of:

- Identifying and learning from mistakes

- Using trial and error

- Setting and then implementing relevant targets

- Putting aside time to think critically about the teaching you do and the lessons you plan

- Responding to the information you receive from students while you are teaching (and marking) in an effort to make your lessons more successful

Here, we will focus briefly on some of the things you can do to ensure your self-reflection is as effective as possible. We have already seen one technique which can aid you in this process (Chapter Five – Reflection – Questions to use when looking back at lessons you have taught). Now I would like to introduce three more.

The first involves the development of a habit. That habit involves asking yourself three questions, twice a day. Once before you start work, and once when you end. The questions are these:

Start of the day:

- What do I hope to improve today?

- How do I hope to improve it?

- Why do I want to improve it?

End of the day:

- What did I improve today?

- How did I improve it?

- Was I right in wanting to improve it?

The most difficult thing here is to get yourself into the habit of asking the questions. Once you have been able to do this, effective reflection will be relatively easy.

You will notice the questions serve to keep your mind trained on this idea of continuous improvement. Asking the first three at the start of every day helps you begin your day's work with the notion of improvement – clearly specified – at the front of your mind. This allows you to maintain a focus on improvement as the day progresses. Something that might otherwise have escaped your attention.

The end of the day questions allow you to look at what you have done during the course of the day in relation to what you set out to do when the day began. It does not matter so much whether or not you did make the improvements you wanted. Rather, the emphasis is on ensuring that you reflect with purpose on what you have been through.

Using this technique ensures every day of your training involves you paying attention to your wider aims and targets, and doing so in a manner which is critical and reflective.

Our second technique involves keeping a diary. This works well for some, but is a turn-off for others. You should decide whether you think it will be to your benefit or not.

Of course, during your training time is likely to be at a premium. Therefore, you need a means through which you can simplify your diary keeping. I would suggest the following:

Write your target at the start of the week and then, on each subsequent day, make a brief note summarising what you have done during the day to achieve that target and indicating what you need to do the following day to build on this. At the end of the week, sit down for ten minutes and read through your entries. This gives you a sense of how far you have gone towards meeting your target and whether or not any significant patterns or trends have developed (for example, you might notice that, unintentionally, you have focussed all week on the things you are already good at, rather than the weaker areas you would really like to develop).

Our third and final reflection technique is medium-term in its focus (as opposed to the two outlined above, both of which are short-term).

Take a copy of the success criteria for your course – that is, the information stating what you need to do to be graded outstanding – in the first few weeks of your training. Read through these and highlight anything which you know you are already capable of achieving. Inevitably, in the first few weeks, this will be little – perhaps even nothing.

Return to the success criteria every couple of weeks and start to highlight those areas in which you are now confident. To increase the sense of progression, you might choose to define a certain level of thickness to indicate the varying security of your confidence. For example:

- Thin line = Mildly confident

- Medium line = Confident

- Thick line = Highly confident

Two points follow. First, you will become familiar with the success criteria for your course. Second, you will be able to visualise your own progress and, by extension, see those areas on which you need to focus.

The technique provides a means through which to maintain a highly reflective attitude through the course as a whole, with this being tied to those things against which you will be judged when your training draws to a conclusion.

Making Observations Effective Part 1 (When you are observed)

Through the course of your training you will be observed on numerous occasions. Primarily, your mentor will conduct these observations. However, it is likely that you will also be observed by other teachers, including members of middle or senior management.

Being observed is a wonderful opportunity to make progress. Having someone with whom to discuss your lesson and who can provide feedback and insight regarding what you planned, how you taught it, and the learning which took place, is invaluable.

Not all observations are the same, though. Nor are all observers equally skilled. The following techniques will help ensure you always get the most out of your observations. They can all be used independently. Some can be used in conjunction.

Specify a focus

Before the observation takes place, tell the observer what you would like them to focus on. For example, you may feel your questioning lacks sufficient rigor. You would then ask them to pay special attention to this during the course of the lesson and, in particular, to examine the extent to which you push students to think more deeply through the questions you ask. At the end of the observation, the observer will be able to provide highly targeted feedback focussing on an area you would like to develop. This raises the efficacy of the observation.

Pre-plan your questions

If you know you are going to be observed, think in advance about what you would like to find out from the observation. Then, plan a series of questions you can ask the observer after the observation has taken place. Here, you are doing two important things. First, you are training your mind to focus on that which matters to you. Second, you are identifying a means (the questions) through which to elicit information about how you are performing in this meaningful area.

Focus on learner outcomes

Through the course of your training period, it is likely that your focus will gradually shift from yourself to your learners. This is natural. At the start of the course, your interest will be mostly taken up with your own performance as a teacher – the process of settling into the role. As time progresses you will come to realise that learner progression is the central goal of all teaching (or you will realise it in a more profound, experiential sense) and that, finding out about what learning has taken place is crucial to effectively assessing the quality of a lesson. As you come to reach this point, ask observers to focus on learner outcomes and to provide feedback on this after observations have taken place.

Identify specific groups of learners

A similar yet subtly different approach involves asking your observer to focus their attention on a specific group of learners. For example, you might ask them to observe what sort of progress less-able students make in your lesson and whether or not the strategies you put in place to support them are effective. When the lesson is over, you can have a useful discussion where you analyse the efficacy of what you did and then speak more broadly about how best to support the group of learners in question.

Tie the observation to your target

Your mentor will know your target. Other observers might not. Ensure observations are tied to your target – what you are seeking to implement – by informing observers in advance. Explain what your target is and what you intend to do to try to achieve it during the course of the lesson. Afterwards, your discussion will centre on whether you achieved this and, if you did not, what you can try next time around to be successful. This will help you to keep focussed on your target and should also give you access to relevant, useful ideas and feedback.

Invite constructive criticism

Constructive criticism is criticism which identifies things which could be changed and then suggests ways in which change might be effected. Ideally, it also specifies what change might look like and why it matters. So, for example, constructive criticism on questioning might identify a problem with a teacher's questioning, explain why this is a problem, suggest how things could be done differently and then provide an example or two of what this might look like in practice. Not all observers are adept at providing constructive criticism. You can help them in their task by asking questions/posing statements such as:

- Tell me one thing I could improve and give me an example of how I could improve it.

- What did you think about X? What could I do to make it better?

- What advice would you give me on how to improve X? Could you give me an example from your own teaching?

Lead the reflection

Our final technique is to make sure that you lead the reflection. Sometimes this isn't necessary. If you have a skilled mentor or observer who understands how to use the process to help you further your development, all will be well. If they are unskilled, however, for whatever reason, you will be better served to take control and direct things to suit your ends. So, for example, you might begin the reflection by stating what you want to focus on, in regard to the lesson you have just taught, and how this relates to your target. Then, through the course of the discussion, you can continue to refer back to this to keep things relevant, useful and on track.

Making Observations Effective Part 2 (When you are observing)

When it comes to observations, the other side of the coin is you doing the observing of more experienced teachers. Here, the aim is to gain an insight into different approaches and effective methods. There is also the opportunity to see things which don't work, or that you would not choose to do yourself. This can be just as valuable as observing good practice.

So let us look at some different techniques you can employ to ensure you get as much as possible from the observations you undertake.

Define a purpose

If your observation has a purpose, it is more likely to prove fruitful. This purpose can be fairly broad – it doesn't have to be specific. For example, it might be to gain a general insight into how a teacher of note deals with a difficult topic. But this is nonetheless a purpose – something to inform your thoughts and actions while you are observing. Inefficient observations tend to involve a teacher sitting in another teacher's lesson without any clear idea of why they are there or what they hope to gain from the exercise. By defining a purpose in advance you can easily avoid this problem.

Specific teachers for specific things

In every school, certain teachers gain a reputation for being good at certain things. One teacher may be lauded for their behaviour management skills, while another teacher may have their praises sung because of their questioning. Finding out who is good at what means finding out who it is worth observing to gain insight into specific areas of pedagogy. If you find yourself struggling with differentiation, go and observe a teacher who is known to be skilled at this. Similar to the previous technique, the aim here is to increase the benefits you can draw from your observation, giving yourself more chance of learning from the time you spend in someone else's classroom.

Observe the learning

When conducting an observation, by all means focus on the teacher and what they are doing, but also take time to focus on the learning. By this, I mean that you should look at what the students do during the course of the lesson. Think about how the teacher structures learning – what they do to make progress happen. As part of this, you can spend time listening to students discussing ideas, as well as reading any work they produce (or watching any performances, if appropriate). This will help you to gain a critical insight into what learning looks like in another teacher's lesson and also how they go about facilitating that learning.

Interact with students

Another useful technique connected to learning involves interacting with students. For some trainee teachers this comes naturally when they are conducting observations. Without hesitation, they will get up and get involved, spending time talking to learners and helping them with their work. If it does not come naturally to you, aim to make it a part of at least some of the observations you do. This gives you a chance to see close up just what kind of learning students are doing. It also allows you access to their knowledge and understanding and, through talking to them and asking them questions, to gain an insight into how this is developing as a result of the learning the teacher has planned.

Observe in response to your own target

You have your target, so why not use this as the basis of your observations? Two paths suggest themselves.

First, you can observe a teacher and spend the majority of that observation analysing what they do that is relevant to your target, how you could take this and adapt it for your own teaching, and whether your understanding of your target is sound, given what you are seeing in this particular lesson.

Second, you can find out which teachers in school are skilled at the thing on which your target is based and then observe them to gain a good insight into how to achieve your aims.

In either case, you should try to discuss the lesson with the teacher afterwards, asking them questions which help you to further identify how you can successfully implement your target.

Look at different groups of students

Every class contains different groups of students. More-able and less-able learners, middle ability learners, students on free school meals, students whose first language is not English, learners with special educational needs and so forth.

Finding ways to support all these different groups is tricky. Effective differentiation takes time to develop. You can speed up the process by focussing your observations on how other teachers work with specific groups of students. As mentioned in the last point, this could involve looking at any teacher you happen to observe, or it could involve finding a teacher noted for their skilful work with certain groups and asking if they are happy for you to see them in action.

Ask why?

Our final technique is called semantic interrogation. This is the process whereby we question the meaning of something, so as to understand it better. For example, a student might come across a new idea and ask why this is taken to be the case. In the process, they would interrogate the meaning of the idea in question, connecting it to their existing understanding at the same time as they subject it to a process of analysis and examination.

When observing a colleague teach, watch what they do, how they structure the lesson or how they interact with students. And then ask yourself 'why?' This is semantic interrogation in action. It sees you going beyond what you see. To get below the surface, you must attribute meaning. In part, this attribution comes through an analysis of the information in front of you. The conclusions you draw can then be tested – either through application in your own teaching, or through discussion with the teacher whose lesson you observed.

With that, we draw this chapter to a close. The message throughout has been a simple one. Outstanding trainee teachers take control of their own development. You can do this by implementing some or all of the ideas outlined above. All that remains is for me to pose a few questions and suggest a few activities to further aid you in this process:

Questions

- Do you find it easy to learn from your own mistakes? Why do you think this is?

- Why do many students develop a fear of failure, making them reluctant to try new things or engage in trial and error? (Consider how most young children have little or no sense of this.)

- In what other learning experiences has trial and error proved helpful? How do these differ from training to teach? How are they similar?

- To what extent would you be prepared to encourage students to embrace and learn from failure in your lessons? How might this manifest itself in practical terms?

- What do you want from your development as a teacher and what do you intend to do to achieve this?

Activities

- Engage in trial and error in a non-teaching based context. For example, pick out a recipe using an ingredient you've never cooked with before or try to make a house of cards four stories high. Whatever you choose, think carefully about the process of learning you go through as you attempt to complete that which you have chosen to do. Finally, consider how the insights you have derived could be applied in the classroom.

- Create your own observation matrix. Start from scratch and identify six categories you think it would be worth looking at when observing someone else teach. Having identified the categories, work out what you would look for in each one as evidence of outstanding practice. You might want to use an existing observation matrix as a starting-point.

- Find a few NQTs (newly-qualified teachers) in your training school. Have a chat with them about their training year. Ask them to tell you how they fared, what steps they took to control their own development and how they went about implementing their targets. Afterwards, reflect on what you can take away from this and use to support your own development.

Chapter Nine – Communicating

As we approach the end of our journey on how to become an outstanding trainee teacher, let us return, for a moment, to the beginning. There we said that one of the answers to the question 'What is teaching all about?' is that teaching is communication.

By this we meant that teaching, at heart, is predicated on the interactions which take place between teachers and students. These interactions rest on communication. That communication is a process of exchange and facilitation; reflecting the twin poles we posited at either end of the continuum in Chapter Six.

Everything you do as a teacher should be viewed, at least in part, through the lens of communication. To do that, you can ask yourself at each step: How effectively am I communicating?

You may also wish to ask yourself a connected question: How effectively am I facilitating communication between students? The latter is important but, I would argue, the former takes precedence.

To that end, this chapter focuses exclusively on how you can ensure your communication is as effective as possible. Employing the techniques and strategies outlined below will help you to refine and improve the manner in which you convey your expectations, explain ideas, pose questions, build rapport and maximise progress. And we will start at the beginning, with the essentials of good communication.

The Essentials of Good Communication

Audience. Purpose. Medium. Message.

Those are the essentials. Whenever you are looking to communicate well, return to these four words and ask yourself if you are confident with each. If you are, your communication will be effective.

Let me provide some analysis of each one.

Audience. Knowing your audience means knowing who you are seeking to communicate with. In the classroom, this means you have an understanding of who your students are, where they are at in terms of their development, what they know, what they don't know, how they are best able to learn, and what engages or motivates them.

If you possess this information, you are in a position to tailor your communication so it fits with the students in question. In short, knowing more about the classes you teach gives you a better chance of communicating with them effectively.

With that said, the simple fact of paying attention to your audience will lead to an immediate improvement in the quality of your planning and teaching. For example, if you think carefully about the type of students in your class and the prior knowledge they possess, then you will be able to use this information to tailor your lesson plan (including the resources) as well as the explanations you give and the questions you ask.

Purpose. By purpose we mean your purpose. What purpose underpins your communication? Identifying and refining your purpose means having a clearer sense of why you are communicating and what you hope to achieve as a result.

We can take much from the book to help us in this aim. First, we can turn to the opening chapters, in which we sought to broaden our understanding of teaching and learning. This development of understanding means we have a clearer sense of what classrooms are all about, as well as a more critical appreciation of what we can do to make ours function well.

In addition, the chapters on lesson planning and facilitation vs. instruction have given us a means through which to think about how we want to teach and why, as well as what we hope to do to maximise progress. Again, this aids us in more clearly defining the purpose of any communication in which we engage.

And here it is worth returning to a point implied above. The communication you do as a teacher includes the resources you create as well as the feedback you give and the teaching you do. At each point of the cycle (planning – teaching – marking), communication is central.

Medium. This leads us onto medium. The medium is the means through which you communicate. It includes your voice, your body (body language), PowerPoint or IWB slides, physical resources, multimedia resources such as videos, and, in music, the sounds you create with instruments.

The medium affects the message. So, for example, explanations provided verbally are qualitatively different from explanations provided in writing on a PowerPoint slide. One brief illustration to secure the point. Consider how the shape of a PowerPoint slide influences the structure of what you communicate through it. Now, compare this to the shape of verbal communication (does it even have a shape?).

When communicating with students, think about how the medium influences your attempts to convey a message. For example, it is often best to deliver written *and* verbal instructions to students at the beginning of a task. This allows students to test their understanding of the former against the latter, giving them confidence they have correctly understood both. Also, through verbal instructions you can inject a sense of pace, whereas with written instructions provide a reminder to which students can refer back during the course of an activity.

Message. Here we have our final essential element of effective communication and, arguably, our most important. The message. That is, the meaning we are seeking to convey.

Having elicited information about our audience, defined our purpose and assessed the media through which we will communicate, we now find ourselves well placed to craft messages which are accessible, relevant and which stimulate learning.

For example, an outstanding teacher may communicate differently with two different classes. This would be predicated on their understanding of the different audiences, their acknowledgement of slightly contrasting purposes and an analysis of which media are likely to be most effective in each case. Through this little bit of prior work, they place themselves in a strong position from which to shape messages which will be accurately understood, sufficiently challenging, connected to prior learning and, as a result, able to stimulate the most learning possible.

To contextualise these points further, observe two teachers in your training school – one who you know is a good communicator and one who perhaps struggles with this side of things. The point is not to develop a critical narrative about the latter. Instead, it is to see in real terms what the contrast is like between the two. This contrast will demonstrate what has been said above. It will also further reinforce the point that paying attention to the essentials – audience, purpose, medium, message – even if it only entails a brief period of thought and analysis, is always preferable to the opposite.

With our groundwork complete, we can spend the rest of the chapter looking at practical examples.

Behaviour Management and Building Rapport

Good behaviour management is built on three things: consistency, high expectations and relationships. We attend to the second of these in a separate section below. Here, our focus is on consistency and relationships.

The future is unknown. We live in the present and have knowledge of the past. If we feel we can predict the future then we tend to feel more at ease with our surroundings. Traditionally, in stable human societies of all shapes and sizes, rules, formal, informal or a combination of the two, help us to do this. They are usually backed by sanctions or consequences of some kind which are applied when the rules are broken.

When it comes to behaviour management, consistency means that students know what to expect. That means it is easier for them to predict the future with a reasonably high level of accuracy. This helps make their experience of your classroom better.

This is not least because they find themselves with a greater chance of behaving in a way that matches or exceeds your expectations. This is much harder to do if you are inconsistent – students will not be able to decide with any degree of confidence whether an action fits with what you want or not.

All this means that, to foster good behaviour management, your communication regarding rules, sanctions and expectations needs to be consistent. If it is, students will quickly come to know what to expect. If it is not, they will remain uncertain. This uncertainty will have a deleterious effect on behaviour in nearly all cases.

Also, if your communication regarding behaviour management is inconsistent, you will find it much harder to exercise authority. The inconsistency which marks your efforts will diminish your capacity to act effectively. For example, if you inconsistently communicate and enforce sanctions, then a student to whom a sanction is eventually applied has every right to question the legitimacy of this application – based as it appears to be on whim or chance, rather than a predictable, rule-based pattern.

Similarly, if you communicate one thing one lesson and one thing the next, students may well question whether you fully understand how to be in charge of the class. For example, let us say that one lesson we allow students to be as loud and as boisterous as they like, then the next lesson we tell them they must work in silence from start to finish. This is likely to arouse surprise and ill-feeling in some students. They will rightly ask the question: Why is today different from last lesson?

So it is vital that, throughout your training year, you seek to communicate behaviour expectations, rules, sanctions and praise as consistently as possible. This might result in some negative experiences in the short-run, such as when students protest or try to challenge that which you are proposing. However, the medium and long-term benefits will be substantial. Students will come to understand what you want and will be able to view their own behaviour through this lens.

We move now to relationships, another essential element of good behaviour management.

Building relationships means building rapport. Rapport is the ability to communicate effectively with individuals or groups. If we do not understand someone, if we know little about them, if we fail to consider their perspective, then rapport will be poor. This has knock-on consequences for our relationship with them.

In the context of the classroom, strong relationships and good rapport means students and teacher see themselves working together towards a common goal.

This is why so much good behaviour management rests on the development and maintenance of positive relationships.

Of course, it is important to remember that your relationship with students should be friendly but never that of a friend. Distance must always be kept. You are the adult and they are the student. The relationship cannot be one of absolute equals, because you are the professional and will need to both exercise your authority and take decisions on occasion which may be unpopular, even if they are in students' best interests.

Here are seven simple ways through which to build rapport with your students:

Ask questions. Did you have a nice weekend? How has your day been so far? What did you think about the homework? We all like to be asked questions about our lives. Such questions signify interest and demonstrate that the question-poser views us as important and worthy of being spoken to.

Listen. Whenever students talk to you, make sure you listen. And listen well. This means paying close attention to what they say and showing that you have listened. You can do this through your body language, by making eye-contact and by responding in a manner which clearly takes account of the content of what they have said. These are obvious points, I know. But, as ever, the frenetic experience of the classroom can often cause us to forget them.

Greet them at the door. If possible, stand at the door of your classroom and greet students as they come in. Ideally, you will have the starter activity displayed on the board so that students can get straight down to work. Greeting students means signalling that you are in charge and in control of the lesson. It is also polite, friendly and indicative of a positive, welcoming attitude.

Model excellent manners. Manners are the gold leaf which gilds the most mundane of interactions. Use them at all times. You will be an excellent model for your students, eliciting positive sentiments and a sense that you recognise the importance of other people's feelings.

Thank them at the end of the lesson. When drawing the lesson to a close, thank your students for their efforts and participation. Once more, this is about finessing relationships by taking the time to publicly acknowledge the importance of your students and the role they play in your teaching. Of course, if a class has behaved poorly it may not be appropriate to thank them. In these situations you should decide whether it will be worth thanking those who have behaved well, or if it would be better to share your disappointment with students and make clear your expectation that matters will improve in the next lesson.

Remain upbeat and enthusiastic. Enthusiasm is infectious. We all warm to positive people. It's as simple as that!

Be firm and direct. This is an extension of the points made earlier about communicating consistency. Being firm means setting clear boundaries and sticking to them. Being direct means communicating with clarity and giving students the information they need to be successful. Cutting out ambiguity makes life easier for students, further predisposing them to you.

High Expectations

Our final area to consider concerning behaviour management and effective communication is that of expectations. And there is only one type of expectation you should have in the classroom: high ones!

We communicate our expectations to students at all times. When we talk to them, when we listen to them, through our body language, through the lessons we plan, the questions we ask and so forth. When planning, teaching and marking we are always and forever communicating our expectations.

And the one simple fact about students that all teachers come to know is that they will almost without fail live up or down to the expectations you communicate. There is little more dispiriting than observing a colleague communicate low expectations to students and then receiving back exactly what they expected.

On the flip side, there is little more rewarding in the job than the feeling which comes from having students consistently meet and surpass your high expectations.

A single example from my own experience. A new Year Nine class came to me one September. I say new because I had never taught any of them before. One lad's name was familiar to me because he had been known in school the previous year for regularly getting into trouble and being disruptive. Here I faced a choice: work from the previous knowledge floating around in relation to his character and behaviour, or ignore it and communicate the same expectations as I had for everybody else.

I chose the latter and, not long after, he was producing excellent work. Throughout the year he was focussed, conscientious and polite. I told him off if his behaviour dipped, praised him for his effort and the good ideas he had and the results were excellent.

I'm no miracle worker. This vignette, while true, could be echoed by tens of thousands of teachers up and down the country. I share only to illustrate the point. All students benefit from high expectations. Some might not reach them; there will be occasions where you feel your high expectations are having no effect. But retaining and maintaining them will always place you and your students at an advantage compared to the alternative.

You can communicate high expectations in everything you do. Dress smartly. Be organised and prepared. Expect these things of students. Make challenge everybody's business. Tell students that you expect everybody to work hard and to apply maximum effort. Praise them when they do. Refuse to accept giving up, I don't know or shoulder shrugging. Do this in a conciliatory, positive way. Give personalised feedback. Provide time in which students can implement it and then draw their attention to the progress they have made. Encourage less-able students to aim for extension tasks. Encourage more-able students to follow independent interests, teach others and write their own super- or hyper-extension tasks.

These are just a few examples of the practical measures you can take.

As a rule of thumb, ask yourself when you are planning, teaching your lessons and marking student books whether or not what you are doing is communicating high expectations. Consider what else you could do to convey this message – and consider what you might need to cut out because, whether intentionally or not, it is undermining this central tenet of your teaching.

Just one more point before we move on. If you are uncertain as to whether or not you accept my point that all students will live up or down to the expectations you set, find the time to observe a student who is perceived as being less-able or difficult to teach in one area yet quite the opposite elsewhere. The experience will be instructive.

Of course, I am not taking responsibility away from the student here. Clearly it is their duty to behave and work hard wherever. But, regardless of where the expectations come from, whether they are solely a result of the teacher's communication or if they are a result of the views the student has about themselves, high expectations will always raise students up in a way that low expectations never will.

Perhaps the starkest demonstration of such a point is the student who looks physically different in one lesson compared to another – their shoulders are no longer hunched, their face is now alert. This physical manifestation of expectation (again, as much the student's as the teacher's) reminds us that we can influence how a student views themselves and their relation to learning through the expectations we communicate.

Inevitably, outstanding behaviour management rests, nearly always, on the communication of high expectations. Make sure it plays a significant part in the messages you convey to the audience in your classroom.

Explaining

In the second half of this chapter we move away from behaviour management towards some of the nuts and bolts of teaching and learning. We will think first about explaining, then questioning before, finally, looking at two communication strategies which can have a big impact on achievement.

Effective explaining is the hallmark of an excellent teacher. Many things need to be explained as part of a lesson: ideas, information, concepts, connections, approaches, what students need to do, problem-solving and so on.

Three simple rules will help you to enhance the quality of your explanations.

First, rehearse your explanation mentally before verbalising it to students or putting it into writing. This helps refine the explanation. It also diminishes the chance the explanation you proffer is misinterpreted by your students.

Second, supplement verbal or written explanations with other sources of information. This will likely be visually and will usually come in the form of images, gestures or a demonstration. Supplementing linguistic explanations with non-linguistic media gives students a chance to access your message through a different form. In addition, it allows them to check they have understood your explanation by comparing the information derived from both sources.

Third, where possible, connect your explanation to students' prior knowledge and experience. This is a simple way to situate what you are explaining within the context of what is already known. Doing this helps students apply their existing understanding to the decoding of your current explanation. It also allows them to make links between that which is new and that which is familiar.

Beyond this, it is well worth exploring a variety of explanation techniques in order to see which work for you. Having a repertoire on which to call means you can adapt your explanations depending on the circumstances in which you find yourself. Here is a non-exhaustive list of different explanation strategies:

- Analogies
- Images
- Diagrams
- Flow-Charts
- Examples
- Worked Examples
- Negative Examples (this is not right because…)
- Exemplar Work (either annotated or not)
- Synonyms and Antonyms
- Metaphors
- Demonstrations
- Instructions
- Step-by-Step Guides
- Practical Experience
- Case Studies
- Stories
- Videos
- Audio
- Crib Sheets

In each case, the purpose is the same, namely, to allow someone else access to that which we know. However, the methods vary and, in so doing, demonstrate(!) the range of options available to us.

When deciding on what explanation strategy you think will be best, return to the essentials of communication outlined above: audience, purpose, medium and message. This helps you to make useful choices quickly and critically. It is also worth noting that using two or three explanation strategies, either simultaneously or consecutively, is a good technique. By doing this, you give students access to your message through a number of different means.

A further technique upon which we can call when seeking to explain things is that of re-explaining. This is where we give our initial explanation before explaining the information again a second and possibly third and fourth time. The aim is to help those students who may have struggled to grasp our initial explanation. To that end, it is generally preferred that the re-explanations become simpler, make use of strategies different to that first employed, or cover a combination of these two points.

The final technique we can consider when it comes to effective explanation is getting students to explain things to one another. For example, we might explain what we want students to do in a given task. Then, we would ask one or two students to re-explain this to the class as a whole. Alternatively, we might explain a new idea, assess which students have grasped it and then ask them to explain it to those students who struggled to comprehend our initial explanation.

Here, the benefit comes from the fact that students listen and talk to each other in a different way to how we listen and talk to them. Having students explain things to one another helps facilitate access to information and ideas by providing a different perspective through which these can be understood.

Questioning

We move now to questioning, an integral part of the teacher's practice. Good questioning almost always leads to good outcomes. Such questioning is effective because the teacher has given thought to how they communicate. This leads them to ask better questions than would otherwise be the case. I have addressed the topic in some detail in my book *How to use Questioning in the Classroom: The Complete Guide.* Here, let me show you five simple techniques you can employ to ensure your questioning hits a consistently high standard.

Open vs. Closed. Closed questions are often useful, particularly when we want to check knowledge, test memory or take the register(!). Open questions provide greater scope, however. They provoke responses which are more discursive and more reliant on reasoning, evidence and example. As such, they involve more thinking. You can use open questions as the basis of a lesson, as lesson objectives, to frame activities and for plenaries. They are also the foundation on which any quality discussion – one-to-one, paired, group or whole-class – rests. In the early stages of your career, it is worth identifying some thought-provoking open questions as part of your planning rather than leaving their construction to the last minute. This way you can start to develop your ability to form and refine high-quality questions of this type.

Might. What is democracy? What might democracy be? The difference is small but instructive. In the first case, knowledge is closed down and the suggestion is that a single answer both exists and should be sought by the respondent. In the second case, knowledge is opened up and made provisional. The implicit message is that many possible answers exist and the respondent should seek to provide one, supporting it through reason and evidence. Inserting the word 'might' into your questions is thus a powerful way to communicate a qualitatively different expectation regarding the type of answers you would like.

Justification. Communicating an expectation that all answers must be justified means students come to understand that assertions are not acceptable as a form of knowledge. This means that, whenever you ask a question, students are under no illusions as to what they should be providing in response. Not just an answer, but an answer predicated on reasoning. Getting students into the habit of justifying their answers takes time. Persistence brings great rewards though. Far more thinking will take place than would otherwise be the case. And students will also spend more time articulating their thought processes. This means you gain access to useful information about what they know and understand at the same time as they have the chance to refine, edit and reflect on their own thoughts.

Question Stems. These are the procedural parts of questions: the bits that come before the subject. Simple examples include: who, what, where, when, why and how. More complex examples include: to what extent…, do you agree that…, is it possible to argue…, why might someone think… and so forth. Familiarising yourself with a range of question stems appropriate for the subject and/or age group you teach means giving yourself a useful box of tools. Whenever a question is required, be it while you are teaching or while you are planning, you will be able to turn to this box, take out a relevant question stem and use it as the basis for a great question.

Questions at the Door. We mentioned earlier how greeting your students makes a very positive statement; that this is a really good technique through which to communicate positivity and high expectations. You can develop this technique by asking students challenging questions as they walk into the room. Doing this gets students thinking about the learning and also communicates a clear message: in this room we are focussed on developing our knowledge and stretching our understanding. It may not be appropriate to do this at the start of every single lesson, but it is certainly worth using it on a regular basis.

Opening Up Success Criteria

Let us now turn to the two communication strategies we can employ to help raise achievement. The first of these is called opening up success criteria. The second (see below) is modelling.

Success criteria are those things students need to fulfil if they are to be successful. Every task has a set of success criteria.

Making these explicit means giving students a better chance of being successful.

Put simply, if we know what we need to do to succeed then we can focus our efforts effectively. The flipside is that, if we don't know what we need to do to succeed – or if this information remains implicit – then it is harder for us to be successful.

You can communicate success criteria in a number of ways. Before you do though, it is important you understand what success looks like in a given lesson or task. This includes identifying what higher and lower levels of success look like, reflecting the fact that not all students will produce work of the same standard. In addition, you should make sure your success criteria are suitably challenging yet sufficiently achievable to stimulate good outcomes. This takes us back to our earlier points about consistently communicating high expectations.

Here are a range of ways in which you can open up success criteria:

- Self- and peer-assessment. By taking part in the process of assessment and looking critically at work (their own or someone else's) students gain an insight into what success requires.

- By displaying them on the board or on slips of paper during tasks. Students can then refer to these while completing the activity.

- By verbally explaining them to students at the start of the lesson and/or at the start of tasks.

- By providing exemplar work which shows how the success criteria can be met. You can annotate such work to provide students with a clearer insight.

- Through modelling of what success looks like. This modelling can be verbal or visual. It can also include modelling of the type of thought processes in which students need to engage to be successful.

- Through providing checklists to which students can refer while they are working. Checklists can be in the form of questions or statements. They can be task-specific or more general. In the latter case, for example, we might give students a checklist for effective non-fiction writing which we ask them to refer to every time they create work of this type, regardless of the topic.

In conclusion, by finding ways to effectively communicate the success criteria against which students' work will be judged, you are giving your learners a much greater chance of channelling their efforts in the right direction. This helps to raise achievement.

Modelling

This is something we have already mentioned on a number of occasions. Here, we will draw our disparate thoughts together and provide some general examples you can call on in your own teaching.

Modelling means showing students what you want them to do or how they might go about doing something in order to be successful. It includes:

- Demonstrating how you want students to engage with a task

- Showing students how to think about a certain topic

- Showing students what a successful piece of work might look like

- Demonstrating how to apply a particular thought process, such as problem-solving, to a given situation

- Showing students what something means

In each case, we are calling on the findings of social learning theory. This states something with which we are all familiar, but whose efficacy can often be overlooked in the classroom:

We all learn through observation and imitation.

In fact, this is an extremely powerful way through which we learn. It is not the only way, granted, but it is an important one.

Outstanding teachers help their students to access ideas, information and ways of thinking by regularly modelling these as part of their everyday teaching. This results in effective communication. The conveyance of information, in all its forms, is enhanced through the provision of models – verbal, written or visual – which students can copy, imitate, internalise and develop.

If you take this into account when planning, when marking and, most importantly, while you are teaching, then good things will quickly follow. Not least a high level of achievement from your students.

We conclude, for the penultimate time, with some questions and activities to help you reflect on the contents of the chapter.

Questions

- To what extent do you already pay attention to your communication with students?

- When you were at school, which teachers were able to build supportive, positive relationships with you and your peers? How did they do this?

What techniques did they call on? And what can you take away from this and use yourself?

- What would you like to characterise the atmosphere in your classroom? Choose three words which sum up the kind of atmosphere you want. How can you communicate this to your students?

- Why are some questions better than others? Justify your answer.

- When was the last time you learned something through modelling? Were you aware the process was taking place?

Activities

- Walk around school during break or lunchtime. Observe how teachers are communicating with students. Think about the messages they are conveying, whether good, bad or indifferent. Use this observation as a basis through which to reflect on the extent of our non-verbal communication, and the influence (perhaps unheralded) which this can have while we are teaching.

- Watch some skilled questioners at work on YouTube. Chat show hosts (some), journalists, political interviewers and barristers are all good examples to which you can turn. Think about how the questions they ask influence the tenor and content of the responses they receive. Having done this, reflect on how you could apply your findings to your own questioning.

- Select four or five difficult or challenging ideas connected to your area of expertise. Work out how you could model these for students visually, verbally and through writing. In each case, consider what approach would best help students to access and then imitate the information you are seeking to convey.

Chapter Ten – From A to B – Creating the Environment for Progress

In this, our final chapter focussing on what you need to do to become an outstanding trainee teacher, we look at a theme which has run throughout the book. That theme is progress, variously described as maximising learning and raising achievement.

When we teach, we want to help students to learn. The learning they do is the progress they make. The better placed we are to help them learn, the more progress they will make. Of course, it is not necessarily the case that progress will be immediately apparent within every single lesson. Rather, we are likely to see evidence of learning within any particular lesson, alongside evidence of progress across a series of lessons. This reflects the fact that progress is inevitably uneven and rarely, if ever, uniform in nature.

At the same time, it indicates that progress can be measured, though the measurement will not always be a summative assessment of what students can do in an exam or test. More often, it will be a qualitative judgement made by you, the teacher. One which takes into account what students could do, what they can now do, and what they need to do to improve.

However we conceive of it, progress remains our aim. We know our lessons have had a positive impact if students know more, understand more and can do more than was previously the case. Everything discussed and exemplified in the book thus far will help you to make great progress a standard feature of your lessons. In what follows, I will draw together some further ideas and tools on which you can call and which we have not yet had cause to fully examine.

Behaviour Management Revisited

In the last chapter, we looked at various ways through which you can start to develop positive behaviour management in your classroom. It is worth us thinking a little more about this here, seeing as how good behaviour and student engagement is vital if we want to facilitate great progress.

In a classroom where behaviour is poor, two things follow. First, students are not directing their focus onto the learning. Second, the scope of what the teacher feels it possible to achieve is diminished.

Both these points inhibit learning, leading to lower achievement as well as a less enjoyable and productive experience for both teacher and students.

In the first case, time is not used effectively and students fail to apply the effort of which they are capable in the direction the teacher desires. In the second case, the teacher lowers their expectations and starts to plan lessons which are predicated on the assumption (based on prior experience) that only certain things are possible with the class in question.

Ideally, we want to be in a situation where students are focussed on learning from the start of the lesson until the end. Where they are actively engaged with the content and applying their effort in pursuit of mastery. We also want to feel that the relationship between us and them is sufficiently good that we can attempt a range of activities and other teaching and learning interventions, confident in the knowledge that students will respond positively.

Everything previously outlined can help you to achieve these aims. In addition, the following will prove of use.

Training students in activities. This means selecting a range of activities which you then use repeatedly over a term or longer. Doing this allows you to train students in how to engage with the activities in question. As a result, they can engage with the learning inherent to the activities increasingly effectively.

We can also note that, when you first introduce students to a new activity, the results are unlikely to be as good as when they are familiar with how that activity works. During the course of your training, when you are trying out a range of different activities, be aware that this very act can itself make behaviour management a little trickier. This should not discourage you from trying things out. You must do this in order to learn and to build your repertoire. However, being aware in advance of the potential consequences is always helpful.

Focussing on the small things. If you do this, the big things are far less likely to enter into the picture. So, for example, if you pull students up on not producing a piece of written work that is as good as it can be, or on their failure to concentrate for the full course of an activity, the discussion and the area for change will centre on this. If you ignore the small things, that ground shifts to bigger things, such as refusing to start the written work or actively seeking to disrupt an activity.

This point harks back to our earlier thoughts concerning high expectations. One way we can communicate high standards, and thus make these a norm in our classroom, is by focussing on the small things. A caveat is that when doing this you should try to avoid coming over as petty. This can be detrimental to rapport, getting in the way of positive relationships.

Minimising transitions. Transitions are the points at which you move from one activity to another. For example, if we have a starter activity followed by feedback followed by an explanation of the lesson followed by an introduction to the main activity followed by students starting that activity, then we have four transitions. Each transition is an opportunity for the pace to slow and for off-task behaviour to develop.

Two points suggest themselves. First, avoid planning lessons which contain a high number of transitions. Second, when you do have a transition, aim to finesse it such that there is little evidence available to students that a transition is taking place. For example, you might display the instructions for the first activity on the board at the same time as you talk through the content of the lesson. This avoids having to stop talking, change slides and then resume.

Building up slowly. When training there is a great temptation to want to do everything at once. Becoming a teacher is exciting and we are keen to try out all our ideas as soon as possible. Try to resist this temptation if you can. Instead, aim to build up slowly. Begin by focussing on one idea you want to try, then introduce a second, a third, a fourth and so on.

Working in this way lets you to build firm foundations. It also stops your attention being overwhelmed while you are teaching. If you try to do everything at once, it is almost inevitable that behaviour will suffer. Students will have too much on which to concentrate and you will be juggling so much that you might not have enough time and energy free to build a positive classroom atmosphere.

Starting out strict. The old phrase goes: Don't smile until Christmas. I wouldn't go this far myself! But the truth embodied in the sentence is worth remembering. It is easier to start out strict and then wind things in than it is to start out soft and attempt the reverse.

Being strict doesn't mean being rude, abrupt or seeking to instil a sense of fear in your students. Far from it.

It simply means being firm and assertive from the word go, focussing on the small things and ensuring you do not let anything slide. As you do this, you can communicate to students why such an approach is important (to keep learning as the centre of attention and to establish an environment in which everyone can succeed). This will give meaning to your actions and ensure students understand that what you are doing is firmly based on helping and supporting them.

Establishing Norms

We move now to think about the norms of your classroom. Norms are unwritten rules of behaviour. They are rules rarely articulated but widely understood. For example, it is a norm in the supermarket to queue up at the checkout and wait your turn, just as it is a norm to eat with a knife and fork at the dinner table. These unwritten rules underpin how we behave in social situations.

So, what are the norms in your classroom? Or, to put it another way, what do you want the norms in your classroom to be?

These questions are important. If you spend time considering the norms you would like to cultivate, you will be in a position to direct your efforts and energies towards successfully establishing these. If you do not do this thinking in advance, you will find the process of creating an excellent environment for progress more difficult.

Let us look at an example to illustrate the point.

Prior to starting our training we decide that one of the norms we want to establish in our classroom is that people should listen actively to one another. This means that they will show each other they are listening through their body language, that they will pay attention, make eye contact and ask relevant questions.

With this norm in mind, we can start to do things while we are teaching which will help to establish it. We might communicate a set of rules to our students, model active listening for them, praise good examples of the norm being followed and admonish behaviour which confounds our expectations.

All of this helps to establish the norm. And the process will be much quicker than if we don't know what norms we want or why we want them.

Most outstanding teachers have a clear understanding of what norms they expect students to adhere to in their classrooms. They then communicate this to their learners and work hard to ensure their expectations become a reality. This, in turn, helps them to secure excellent outcomes because their classroom comes to function in a way they have predetermined will be beneficial to all.

Here are five steps you can work through to identify and then establish the norms you want.

Step 1: Overview

First, sit down and think about the general norms of behaviour you want to see in your classroom. These are the unwritten rules you want students to follow all or most of the time. They might include things such as treating others respectfully, applying effort in every activity, and not giving up when faced with challenges.

Step 2: Specifics

Next, think about the specific norms you would like to see. By specific we mean specific to certain situations. So, for example, how do you want students to come into the lesson? How do you want them to start the lesson? What do you want them to do when taking part in certain activity types such as speaking and listening? Here we are thinking about how your general norms will play out in specific settings.

Step 3: Communication

Having done this, reflect on how you will communicate these norms to students. This is particularly important at the start of your time working with a class. They will not be familiar with the norms you want and will only come to know these if you convey them. You might choose to go down a more formal route involving written rules, or you might go for a less formal option focussing on modelling and verbal explanation. The second part of this step happens in the lesson, when you put into practice the communication strategies you have decided on in advance.

Step 4: Praise

An excellent tool through which to establish and maintain the norms you want is praise. Praising the behaviour of students who follow your norms sets up a positive role model other students can copy. It draws attention to the behaviour you want and reinforces this by conditioning students to associate good things (praise) with the carrying out of the desired norms.

Step 5: Sanctions

The flipside of praise. If students break the norms you are seeking to establish, sanctions need to be applied. Otherwise, a sense is likely to develop that there is no consequence to behaving in a way counter to that which you desire. Sanctions include the withholding of praise, admonishment of behaviour and non-verbal gestures such as frowns and head shaking. They can escalate to things such as detentions if the situation warrants it.

Concluding this section we can say that creating the environment for progress rests in part on the establishment of norms, at your behest, which allow progress not only to take place, but to be maximised. To do this effectively you should consider what norms you want to see in your lessons and then communicate this information to students. Finally, you should consistently use praise and sanctions (perhaps favouring the former over the latter) to ensure your norms are maintained throughout the course of your teaching.

The Values of Your Classroom

Values are the beliefs which underpin our actions. They are the things we think are important. Most norms are informed by certain values we hold. For example, the norm of greeting people when we first see them stems, in part, from the fact that we value politeness, friendship and respect.

As with the norms of your classroom, the values are set by you. If you do not set them, or if you do so in a perfunctory way, you are less likely to be successful than if you sit down and define what it is you want to underpin the lessons you teach and the learning students do.

To some extent, the values of your classroom will depend on the subject and/or age-group you teach. This reflects the fact that certain things are privileged in certain subjects and in relation to certain stages of children's and young people's development.

The first step towards defining your values is to think about why you chose to train as a teacher in the first place and what you hoped to achieve by entering the profession. Many people join because they see the job as inherently rewarding, with this reward coming from the simple fact you're your working life involves helping and supporting others.

Once you start down this road of reflection you will quickly come to the central values animating the choices you have made. These can then form the basis of the values you want to see echoed in your classroom.

The next step is to add to these any values you think it important students learn and gain experience of. Here we are thinking about our wider role as teachers. That is, to socialise children and young people into good ways of acting and thinking. This reflects the moral dimension of learning which forms part of the hidden curriculum (that which is taught but which is not prescribed by the formal curriculum, which consists of knowledge, understanding and skills).

Finally, we need to think about the values which, when enacted, will help us to create an environment in which learning is central and in which, therefore, progress is maximised.

It may be the case that the three sets of values you define overlap. You will probably be able to shrink them down to a core set which, taken together, reflect your own beliefs about teaching, the things it is important for students to learn as they grow older, and the things which contribute to good learning and good outcomes.

Having been through this process, you will have a selection of values you can use to inform every decision you make as a professional. This is particularly useful when you have a tricky decision in which the path forward is not clear. Such a path can be identified by looking at the choices open to you through the lens of your values. In doing this you will be able to make a judgement which fits with your core aims.

Another benefit of defining your values is that you then have something to which you can refer in times of trouble. If a lesson goes wrong, if you feel weighed down by your work, if you just can't quite seem to achieve a target…In all these cases, by going back to the values you earlier defined you will be able to reset yourself, remind yourself why you are doing the training and, through this process, help yourself to be successful.

Thus, having a clear set of values in place makes dealing with difficulties easier. And, of course, this is a message you can communicate to your students. Doing so will provide them with a tool – a way of thinking – from which many benefits can flow, as we have seen.

In terms of progress – our guiding theme in this chapter – everything outlined above concerned with the impact your values will have on your decision-making and so forth will contribute to your being able to maximise the learning students do in your lessons.

Effective Marking

Our last two sections have been, necessarily, reflective in nature. Norms and values, while important, involve us thinking about the structure of our classroom environment and the concepts which underpin this. Here, and in our next section, our focus will be a little more practical in nature. We will be demonstrating techniques which apply some of the thinking outlined above. First we will at marking, then at feedback.

The two are closely connected. Marking involves the provision of feedback, after all. Separating them out allows us to view each one through a clearer lens.

Beginning with marking then, we can say three things:

- Effective marking helps students to make progress.

- Students need opportunities to implement the information conveyed through your marking.

- In general, when it comes to marking, less is more (and by this, we mean marking less frequently but more deeply).

As such, marking plays a central role in helping students to make progress. It is through marking that you are able to gain a sense of where your students are at, what they understand and what they are capable of. But so too is it an opportunity for you to give them the information they need to make improvements.

Thus, marking is about eliciting and using information. We elicit information about what our students think, know and can do. Then we use this information to inform our planning and to help them to improve.

Formative vs. Summative

Marking is commonly divided into two types: formative and summative. Formative marking is where we give students qualitative information explaining what they have done well and what they need to do to improve. Summative marking is where we sum up a student's learning, presenting this information in a quantitative form such as a number, mark or grade. Both are important.

You should regularly mark students' work summatively and record these grades in your mark-book. This will let you track progress over time (see below). However, students generally learn much more from formative marking. Such marking contains useful information in a way that grades, levels or marks don't. Here we can illustrate the point:

Summative Marking: 65%

Formative Marking: Rebecca, your essay contains a range of examples you have used to effectively illustrate your points. You have also given a conclusion which sums up the arguments before clearly stating what you think and why. To improve, you should try to use a wider range of keywords. This will help to make your writing more academic, which is what the examiner is looking for.

Formative feedback is feedback which helps students to learn.

Summative feedback is feedback which sums up what students know.

A good rule of thumb is to give students regular formative feedback, to always record summative marks in your mark-book and to share the latter with students at pre-determined points in the year. This way, you keep their focus on applying effort in pursuit of improvement.

Recording and Tracking

This is an important aspect of marking, one which will play a bigger role in your working life after your training year, when you have your own classes to teach for an extended period of time.

Still, it is worth getting to grips with it as soon as possible.

You will need a mark-book. Some teachers prefer a physical one, others opt for an Excel spreadsheet. In this you should record the marks, grades or levels you give students for various pieces of work.

The major benefit here is that you can analyse your mark-book over time to see what trends and patterns develop. You can then use this information to make interventions. For example, a particular student might plateau over the course of a few months, while the work of a second may demonstrate a decline in achievement. In both cases, the information in your mark-book will give you grounds to act. Through your intervention you will be able to improve matters and, in turn, maximise student progress. This will be harder to achieve if you are not recording marks for student work.

Constructing Assessments

When constructing assessments, you should think carefully about what you want students to produce for you to mark. Ideally, you will want pieces of work which are rich in detail and sufficient in size and scope to give you an accurate insight into the learning in which students have engaged.

Assessment pieces can be formal things such as tests, essays and so on. Or they can be more informal products on which students work individually, in pairs or in groups. Essentially, an assessment piece is whatever you define as an opportunity for students to demonstrate their learning. Therefore, it is incumbent on you, if you want to be an outstanding trainee teacher, to design opportunities in which students will be able to showcase the full range of their powers.

A second point to consider is whether you want to build into your assessment pieces ways and means through which you can test students' knowledge and understanding for common misconceptions. For example, if you have taught a topic in which a certain idea is frequently misunderstood, you might then choose to include a specific question connected to this as part of the assessment. Here we are directing students in order to elicit information we think will prove particularly helpful in our assessment of their present abilities.

Identifying what you are marking for

When marking, it is helpful to know what you are looking for. This saves time and increases your effectiveness. Being able to do this is partly a result of experience. However, there are two techniques you can employ from the very beginning of your training.

First, refer back to the objectives and outcomes which shaped the lessons you taught. While marking students' work, look to see whether or not there is evidence they have met these.

Second, use the success criteria you have opened up for students during lessons (see the previous chapter). Reminding yourself of these before you start to mark will make the process much simpler.

Of course, it goes without saying that in many cases you will also have external mark-schemes or criteria you can use to help you mark. Nonetheless, the two strategies above will always prove useful.

Marking Regularly

We said earlier that marking at is most effective tends to be done less often but to a deeper level. This does not mean that it is done irregularly. Far from it. In fact, making sure you mark student work on a regular basis is imperative if you want to keep on top of where they are at and to consistently communicate what they need to do to improve.

So you will need to decide what regular means to you. When doing this, you should look to strike a balance between gaining a frequent insight into student thinking and making sure that the marking you do has an impact. If you mark too often, students will not have a chance to implement the feedback you give them. Furthermore, you will find it difficult to discern what progress they are making. This is because you will be too close, failing to allow sufficient distance from which to accurately observe progress.

Effective Feedback

We turn now to feedback. If marking is the process, feedback is the content. Marking is what we do. Feedback is what we give.

Formative Feedback

As noted earlier, formative feedback provides students with much more information than summative feedback. This information helps them to understand what they have done well and what they need to do to improve. It opens up success criteria and gives students the guidance they need to make progress.

In general, two or three strengths and one target is the preferred approach. This is for two reasons. First, a higher number of strengths makes it more likely students will engage positively with the constructive criticism. Second, one target is enough. Any more and you are asking students to divide their minds between multiple aims. This diminishes their capacity to act effectively and means their efforts are spread thinly instead of being concentrated on one specific thing.

When students have successfully implemented a target, set them another one. But not until then.

Written Feedback

Feedback can come in different forms. The two most common are written and verbal (with non-verbal being the third type). Written feedback is nearly always a result of the teacher taking in student work, marking it and returning it.

Here are a few pointers for making this as effective as possible.

1. Follow the advice given above.

2. Personalise the feedback by using the student's name. This is motivational, increases relevance and makes it more likely the student will take the feedback seriously.

3. Write clearly. If students cannot read your feedback they will probably ignore it.

4. Give students time to read your feedback, to think about it and to discuss it with you or with a partner.

5. Provide opportunities for students to act on your feedback (for more on which, see below).

Verbal Feedback

Verbal feedback is mostly given during lessons, either to individuals, to groups or to the class as a whole. It is most effective when clear, unambiguous and accompanied by examples or modelling of some kind. During activities, it is generally a good idea to circulate through the room and provide verbal feedback wherever you deem it can help students to make more progress. Some examples include:

- Helping students to think differently about a particular idea

- Stretching and challenging student thinking

- Indicating what is good about the work thus far and why

- Indicating how the work could be improved and why this would be an improvement

- Redirecting students who have gone off-task

An excellent differentiation technique involves trying to talk to every student in your class at least once over the course of a lesson or a series of lessons. Doing this means providing tailored, verbal feedback to every student, helping them to access the work and to make as much progress as possible.

Implementing Targets

We mentioned previously the importance of giving students the opportunity to implement the targets you provide through your feedback.

If no such time is given, the feedback fails in what it is intending to do. Namely, help students to make progress.

With verbal feedback, an opportunity for implementation normally arises naturally – students can do it as soon as you have finished talking and left them to continue with the activity. When it comes to written feedback, however, you need to plan time in your lessons when implementation can take place. Here are five examples of how to do this:

Target Tracker Sheets. Stick a sheet into the front of students' books and ask them to record their targets in here. At the start of the lesson or at the start of relevant activities, ask students to return to this sheet and to remind themselves of what their current target is. They should then try to put this into practice.

Starter Implementation. As a starter activity, hand back the work you have marked, ask students to read your feedback and then challenge them to select a section of their work and to redo it in accordance with the target you set.

Write/Do/Reflect. Students write their target at the top of a piece of work, complete the work while trying to implement their target, and then write a reflective paragraph at the end focussing on whether they have achieved their goal or not.

Mid-Lesson Reviews. Ask students to remind themselves of their target at the start of the lesson. Half-way through the lesson, draw proceedings to a halt and lead a mid-lesson review. This should last around 3-5 minutes and should involve students assessing to what extent they have worked to implement their targets during the course of the lesson – and what they intend to do about this in the time that remains.

Homework. Set students homework tasks which focus on them implementing their targets. While this relies on students completing the homework(!), if done effectively it can have a significant impact on progress.

And with those final thoughts we draw our last chapter to a close, leaving only the conclusion ahead of us. For the final time then, let me present you with a selection of questions and activities to help you reflect on the theme of progress and some of the specific ideas we have looked at in this chapter.

Questions

- What does progress mean to you in your subject or age-group? What do you think it will look like and how will you know if it is as great as you want it to be?

- If we plan and teach good lessons, mark regularly and provide relevant feedback, will progress take care of itself? Why?

- Have I made too much of maximising progress? Are there other aims to which teachers should attend? Is privileging progress taking a mechanistic view of the job?

- What sort of feedback have you received during your educational career? When was it helpful and when was it not? What lessons can you take away from this?

- Is it always possible too elicit the information you want from students, regarding their learning? Why?

Activities

- Find a fellow trainee teacher – either from your course or in your training school. Give each other a topic and then plan an assessment activity the other could use. While this activity is tricky, and you might not produce something of great merit, the purpose is to get you thinking critically about the structure of assessment activities and what you need to include or focus on if you are to give students the best opportunities to show the progress they have made.

- Look through students' books when you are observing other teachers. Focus on the marking. Ask yourself what kind of feedback the teacher has given and the extent to which this helps students to make progress. Then, talk to students about the marking and ask them how easy they find it to implement the targets they are set.

- Make a list of strengths and targets you think are common to your subject or age-group. You can then share these with students (they are, after all, success criteria) and use them to help you mark more effectively (and more efficiently!).

Conclusion – In The Beginning There Was The Lesson

So there we have it. How to be an outstanding trainee teacher laid out in full. I hope you've found it useful. I hope it's given you lots of practical ideas you can apply in your classroom. And I hope it's helped you to reflect on what teaching and learning involve, as well as what it means to be a brilliant teacher in a modern education system.

Rather than summing up everything which has been said in the book, I'd like to take this opportunity to draw your mind in a slightly different direction. A pragmatic one, in fact.

In modern societies where labour is divided between masses of different individuals, we have an education system which gives children and young adults the opportunity to access ideas and information at the behest of a trained professional: the teacher. Teachers manage this task by creating lessons.

This, of course, is familiar to us all.

But it can be easy to forget that it is only in our lessons that we have an opportunity to influence our students.

Now how's that for a statement of the bleedin' obvious?!

Yet, this truism is often forgotten. And the consequences which run from it are even more often overlooked.

If we accept that the high point (perhaps the only point) of our influence comes during lessons, then we should also acknowledge that our energies will be most effectively used if saved for this point.

It follows that if you arrive at your lessons tired and exhausted from excessive planning and marking, you will not be able to make efficient use of the most important time available to you: the time you are actually teaching.

Most teachers understand this point, but many do not adapt their behaviour to take account of its meaning. Thus, burnout is a frequent problem in the profession, with teachers entering the classroom shattered due to the amount of time they have spent marking every inch of every book or trying to plan the perfect lesson.

Such behaviour is well-intentioned. But it is also self-defeating. To be consistently outstanding in the classroom, you need to have plenty of energy to hand every time your students walk through the door. This means you need to look after yourself. You need to rest, relax and sleep well. You need to eat properly, leave work at a decent time and not spend every evening and weekend marking and planning.

It goes without saying that there will be times when you have no choice, but so too will there be lots of times when a choice is available. And that choice needs to be made through the prism of a question: What will benefit my students the most? Will it be the perfect lesson I spent three hours planning? Will it be the book marked to within an inch of its life, covered in notes and annotations? Or will it be me, full of energy, interacting and leading students to the best of my abilities during our lessons together?

The answer will always be the latter.

Remember this through your training – remember it through your career. The maximum impact you can have on your students is while you are actually teaching them. So save your energy for that time.

Plan great lessons, but don't over-plan. Don't aim for perfection. It doesn't exist. Aim for great and then know that, by using your energy while you deliver the lesson, you will be able to elevate it to an even higher standard.

Mark books, give formative feedback, but don't over-mark and don't give masses of feedback. Think about how to be effective and efficient. Mark significant pieces of work which show you all the learning students have done in one go. Give clear, precise feedback which centres on one target students need to implement to improve. When they've succeeded in doing this, give another target, and so on.

Once again, keep in mind that the most effective use of your energy is when you are in the classroom, working with your students. So don't use all of it up outside lessons.

To reinforce the sense of these concluding remarks, consider how you feel when you are tired and teaching a lesson. The difference compared to when you are teaching and full of beans is palpable. What you can do, how effectively you can make decisions, how attentively you can follow the progress students are making: each of these is diminished by tiredness.

And it is a downward sloping curve. The more tired you are, the more significant the drop in your abilities.

So, while training, while pursuing your highly successful career in education, while become outstanding, be sure to remind yourself that the classroom is the place where the magic happens – and that to maximise the magic, you need to have your energy levels as high as possible.

Here endeth the lesson(!)

Select Bibliography

You can find a list of my books and (free) resources at the front. Here is a select bibliography of excellent books connected to teaching, learning and education you might also like to take a look at.

Paul Black, et al, *Assessment for Learning: Putting it into Practice*

Guy Claxton, *Building Learning Power*

Carol Dweck, *Mindset*

Andy Griffith and Mark Burns, *Outstanding Teaching: Engaging Learners*

Paul Ginnis, *The Teacher's Toolkit*

John Hattie, *Visible Learning*

Doug Lemov, *Teach Like a Champion*

Geoff Petty, *Teaching Today*

Geoff Petty, *Evidence-Based Teaching*

Bill Rogers, *Classroom Behaviour*

Jim Smith and Ian Gilbert, *The Lazy Teacher's Handbook*

Isabella Wallace and Leah Kirkman, *Pimp Your Lesson*

Printed in Great Britain
by Amazon